GOOD
HOUSEKEEPING

THE ULTIMATE KIDS CHRISTMAS BOOK

Crafts, Recipes & Fun!

GOOD
HOUSEKEEPING

THE
ULTIMATE
KIDS
CHRISTMAS
BOOK

Crafts, Recipes
& Fun!

kids
HEARST
HOME

Workshop

# of Contents

Introduction

AS A KID, I *loved* all the excitement leading up to Christmas—the anticipation of stockings and my cousins arriving; watching our favorite holiday movies and eating warm sugar cookies fresh from the oven; and the piles of wrapped presents!

At Good Housekeeping we wanted to capture the spirit of the holiday in an awesome, celebratory book for you to enjoy every year. So we asked ourselves, for a kid what makes Christmas, *Christmas*?

There are the festivities, of course. (Not to mention time off from school.) In Chapter One, Celebrate, we explore how kids around the world celebrate Christmas. (For some, the holiday season starts in September; for others, it involves fish in bathtubs!) We uncover the history of the most beloved Christmas trees and ornaments and include plenty of festive facts too. (Did you know that Chandler, Arizona, is home to a towering tumbleweed Christmas tree? What's a tumbleweed Christmas tree? Turn to page 45!) Plus, our Choose Your Own Advent-ure activities—and fun ideas like holiday movie marathons, books to read, and gift swap how-tos—will make every day of December a celebration.

Christmas also wouldn't be Christmas without the dazzling decorations. In Chapter Two, Craft, you'll find simple projects for creating DIY holiday delight. Trim your tree with handcrafted ornaments, personalize your stocking with your own designs, find clever ways to use candy canes, or deck your halls with cool and colorful wreaths. Plus, you'll find ways to wrap your special gifts for family and friends. Bring on the holiday spirit!

Finally, the sweetness of the season is thanks, in part, to its delicious treats. In Chapter Three, Bake, you'll find 55 easy-to-make Christmas confections and desserts to fill Santa's sleigh—frosted snowmen cupcakes, carol-inspired cake pops, and cookies galore, all tested-till-perfect by the chefs in the Test Kitchen. Whether you're baking for family, school friends, or Santa, you'll find something for everyone.

Ultimately, Christmas is Christmas because of the time we spend together and the joy we bring one another. The real presents are the meaningful experiences and memories we share. This book will serve up holiday cheer every time you open it—and will inspire you as you make your time together magical.

Happy holidays, from our homes to yours!

Jane

Jane Francisco
EDITOR IN CHIEF

Chapter One
CELEBRATE

Discover exciting holiday traditions from around the world.

Australia

Christmas in the summer? Yep!
Because Australia is in the southern hemisphere, its seasons are the opposite of North America's. In fact, Aussies often celebrate Christmas Day by going to the beach and holding backyard barbecues. Legend has it that Santa lets his reindeer rest once arriving in Australia and puts kangaroos to work pulling his sleigh.

DOWN UNDER

Austria

If you thought coal in your stocking was bad, think again. In Austria, St. Nicholas brings gifts to good kids while Krampus—a half-man, half-goat figure—comes around to drag the bad kids away. Yikes! Some towns even hold an event called Krampuslauf, in which fathers dress up as the fabled goat-man and parade through the streets, warning kids to behave. Make sure you're good for goodness' sake!

Brazil

Christmas pageants called os pastores (Portuguese for "the shepherds") are an important part of the holiday season. These are like Nativity plays, with one very important difference: A shepherdess tries to steal the baby Jesus. Luckily, she never succeeds!

Like the Aussies, Brazilians celebrate Christmas during the summer. Some say Santa sheds his fur-trimmed red suit for a cooler silk one here. Don't forget your shades, St. Nick!

THE *First Christmas*

Christmas celebrates the birth of Jesus Christ, who was born almost 2,000 years ago in the town of Bethlehem. In Christianity, Jesus is believed to be the son of God. The word *Christmas* is a combination of "Christ" and "Mass" and means the holy festival of Christ. Each year on Christmas Eve, churches mark the holiday with children's plays and pageants that depict the Nativity story.

Ethiopia

In Ethiopia, people celebrate Christmas, called Genna, on January 7. Ethiopians don't typically exchange gifts to celebrate Genna. Instead, the holiday is a time for church visits and sports. One sport is so closely tied to Christmas that it's called Genna. According to legend, shepherds played it to celebrate the birth of Jesus. Today entire towns gather for Genna matches, which feature curved, wooden sticks, a wooden ball, and two goals. It's like field hockey but far more festive.

France

If you're in France on Christmas, make sure to get an invite to Le Réveillon de Noël, what the French call Christmas Eve and celebrate with a big meal. Even if the main course of roasted goose, oysters, smoked salmon, and foie gras (made from duck liver) isn't to your taste, the dessert probably will be. Bûche de Noël is a thin sponge cake rolled and frosted to resemble a Yule log.

Sweet tooth still not satisfied? Head to Provence, where 13 desserts are traditionally served on Christmas Eve, symbolizing Jesus and his 12 disciples. All the treats are made from fruit, nuts, and pastries.

Germany

Many U.S. holiday traditions, including Christmas trees and Advent calendars, originated in Germany. At Germany's many outdoor holiday markets in town squares, you can buy Christmas gifts and winter treats like roasted almonds and gingerbread hearts. The most famous Christmas market is in the city of Nuremburg. It features blown-glass ornaments and visits from Christkind, an angel with blond ringlets who brings gifts to young children.

Greece

In the seafaring country of Greece, people decorate boats for Christmas. Yes, boats! The Feast of St. Nicholas—the patron saint of sailors (and many others)—takes place on December 6. On this day, Greeks mark the beginning of the holiday season by covering boats of all sizes, from dinghies to ships, in twinkle lights. At home, they make small paper boats, called *karavaki*, to adorn fireplaces and doors. Children also go door-to-door singing holiday carols with a karavaki, which neighbors fill with candy. Sounds a bit like trick-or-treating, don't you think?

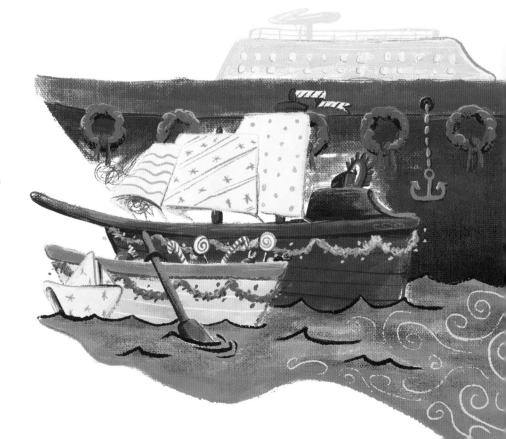

Iceland

Twelve days of Christmas? Iceland does one better and celebrates for 13 days. Starting on December 12 and each night leading up to Christmas, Icelandic children are visited by one of the 13 Yule lads. Kids place their shoes near a window before heading to bed. In the morning, they'll find their shoes filled with candy if they were good or rotten potatoes if they were bad.

Italy

If you have a Nativity scene in your home, that's a slice of Italy.
The first one is believed to have been displayed by St. Francis of Assisi in 1223. Since then, Italians have upped their Nativity game, including objects like houses, waterfalls, and foods in their displays. Naples has become famous for including modern celebrities. You might even find statues of Elvis Presley or Cristiano Ronaldo among the wise men and shepherds.

That's not the only part of Italian Christmas that's over the top. They have four gift givers throughout the season: St. Lucia, baby Jesus, Santa Claus, and Befana. The last one is a grizzled witch who leaves sweets or coal in a stocking, depending on how children have behaved.

Mexico

In Mexico and many other Latin American countries, there's no such thing as a good night's sleep on Christmas Eve. The event is known as Nochebuena, which means "good night." It lives up to the name as families, and sometimes entire towns, gather for grand feasts (tamales and a pork dish called lechón are often on the menu), followed by singing and dancing into the wee hours. Children get in on the fun, swinging at piñatas stuffed with candies and trinkets. Christmas or bust!

Philippines

If you've ever wished Christmas could last a little longer, then try celebrating in the Philippines. The holiday season there is really long—September 1 is the beginning. Stores start playing nonstop Christmas carols, and families decorate their homes with *paróls*, star-shaped lanterns that represent the Star of Bethlehem.

Poland

Gather around to share at a Polish Christmas Eve dinner. Known as Wigilia, the traditional meal begins with the oplatek. The rectangle, paper-thin wafer is about the size of a sheet of construction paper folded in half and made of flour and water. It's stamped with a Nativity image. Everyone at the table breaks off a piece and shares a holiday greeting before passing it along. Sometimes, even pets get pieces of oplatek.

Russia

Because Christmas and other religious holidays were banned by the Soviet Union, New Year's became a more important time for celebration. On Novy God, or "new year," children gather around the holiday tree (yes, they decorate a New Year's tree!) and call for Grandfather Frost and his granddaughter, Snegurochka. When the duo appear, all the lights on the tree magically turn on. Those who've been nice will also find a little pile of gifts beneath the Novy God tree.

Singapore

Singapore has some of the world's most luxurious shopping destinations. During the holidays, these neighborhoods get Yuletide makeovers with spectacular decorations lining every street and storefront. You'll find millions of holiday lights and towering displays, some more than 40 feet high.

Slovakia

People of Slovakia, and other countries in central Europe, enjoy a large freshwater carp for Christmas Eve dinner. Here's where things get, well, fishy. Instead of buying a carp from the grocery store, families catch one and then keep it in their bathtub for several days before the meal. Often kids are charged with looking after it until the day of the feast.

South Africa

South Africans better come hungry for the holidays! Most families get together at a mega Christmas cookout called Braaing. The meal includes a main course of marinated steaks and boerewors (sausages), followed by a dessert of malva (a sweet and spongy apricot pudding) and custard. The country has adopted the practice of putting up evergreen trees, much like the one in your home. But they add a twist: an extravaganza of hand-beaded ornaments.

Sweden

St. Lucia's Day is a special part of the Christmas season in Sweden, as well as in neighboring Finland and Norway. Celebrations involve candlelit processions with the oldest daughter in each family dressed like St. Lucia. The girls serve the family S-shaped "Lucia" buns and coffee or mulled wine while wearing a white gown with a red sash, plus a special crown with greenery and candles. That may sound like princess-worthy attire, but it's not all fairy tales. Those crowns sometimes use electric candles, but when they don't kids often wear a plastic shower cap to keep hot wax from dripping in their hair!

Ukraine

Ukrainians put a creepy, crawly spin on Christmas decor: spiders and spiderwebs. According to a beloved folktale, a poor widow couldn't afford to decorate a tree for her children. Spiders in the house took pity, and the family awoke Christmas morning to a tree adorned with beautiful, glistening webs. Today, Ukrainians use paper and wire to make ornaments resembling the crafty critters. They call these *pavuchky* ("little spiders") in Ukrainian.

United Kingdom

If you're celebrating Christmas in the United Kingdom, get ready for Christmas crackers. No, not the kind you'd pair with cheese. They're prettily wrapped cardboard tubes filled with a paper crown, a small trinket, and a joke printed on a slip of paper. (Think of them as a big, festive take on a fortune cookie.) But wait, there's more: The wrapped cylinders also contain a popping device that makes a crackling sound when they're opened. It's a good laugh and a mini fireworks show all in one.

Choose
YOUR OWN
ADVENT-URE!

IT'S CHRISTMASTIME—and your excitement is probably through the roof. There's no better way to count down to the main event than with an Advent calendar. Developed in 19th-century Germany, these special calendars traditionally have little doors or flaps numbered 1 to 24 (one for every day of December through Christmas Eve) with a small candy or toy behind each. On the following pages you'll find an activity-based take on the tradition with a festive lineup of things to make, see, and do. The countdown is on!

Why do we call it Advent?

Advent means the arrival of a notable person, thing, or event. Christians call the four Sundays leading to Christmas the Advent season, and they have special prayers, readings, and traditions during this time.

1

Bundle up and head outside for a winter walk or hike.

While you're on the trek, gamify it by counting the number of a particular animal or object that you see—say, birds or pinecones. You can also look for objects like sticks, flowers, and rocks to arrange on the ground and form the letters in your name.

Snow Much Fun!

If you're blessed with a blanket of snow this holiday season, try your mittened hand at one of these powdery pastimes.

Ice Castle Contest Take your snow day to new heights! Pack snow tightly in Bundt pans, and see who can create the most epic winter retreat.

Tic-Tac-Snow Draw lines in the snow, then use sticks for Xs and pinecones for Os. A much "cooler" alternative to plain old notebook paper.

Ice Balloon "Egg" Hunt Freeze water balloons (or food-colored ice cubes), and hide them in the yard. See who can find the most before they start to melt. (Up the stakes, and insert a small prize like a jelly bean or a candy mint in the center of the balloons.)

Expert Snow Angel No more annoying pile of snow in the middle of your creation! After completing the standard jumping jack motion, swing your legs (together, as one unit) from left to right. Hug your legs toward your chest, then stand. Voilà—a picture-perfect snow angel.

2 Share the Christmas spirit.

Ensure you're on Santa's nice list, and make people in your community happy by volunteering or doing random acts of kindness. Need inspiration for what to do? See our "Find Your Inner Santa" list on page 52.

3 Whip up a gift that oozes fun: merry slime.

This gooey goodness is equally fun to make, play with, and give to others.

To make:

1. Squeeze 5 ounces of **glue** into a bowl.

2. Add 1 tablespoon **baking soda**.

3. Add a small amount of **glitter paint** in a Christmas color, drop by drop, until you get the shade you want.

4. Stir until combined, then mix in 3 tablespoons of **saline solution**.

5. Roll the slime in your hands until it no longer sticks—this can take as long as 5 minutes. (Hint: If it's still too sticky, add more saline solution.)

6. Finish by folding in **holiday treasures**, such as mini-plastic ornaments, Christmas-themed erasers, or letter beads that spell out a seasonal message like "J-O-Y."

Gift It!
Package slime in small, airtight jars for a homemade holiday gift for friends.

4 Build a blanket igloo.

Whether you want to use it to write your letter to Santa Claus without prying eyes, watch a Christmas movie on a tablet undistracted, or hunker down for a long winter's nap (all the celebrating can be exhausting!), a cozy indoor igloo is the perfect holiday retreat. All you need are some light blankets, spare sheets, beach towels, or tablecloths for your construction.

Add to the wintery charm and hang paper snowflakes along the "roof" of your igloo. (For a step-by-step guide to making your own, see "Winter Wonderland" on page 82.)

the *Table Fort*

Drape several flat sheets over the sides of a dining table and—voilà!—instant blanket bunker. Use heavy books—like dictionaries, atlases, or textbooks—to hold the sheets in place. Need more room? Push the dining chairs out, and extend the sheets over the chairbacks.

the Corner Fort

Transform an unused nook into a three-sided hideout. Secure one corner of a large, lightweight sheet at the intersection of two walls with an adhesive, like masking tape or poster putty. Place chairs or boxes on both sides, and drape the sheet across for an easy escape.

5   Warm up with hot cocoa.

For an easy recipe, plus a festive,
Frosty-inspired topping, see page 169.

6   Turn your house into a holiday scavenger hunt.

See if you can spot all these items in your home—don't forget to look in unusual places like the design on wrapping paper, tree ornaments, your crowded coat closet, or even your sock drawer. Set a timer for 10 minutes, and see how many you can find before the buzzer rings.

✓ Cookie tin	✓ Plaid
✓ Candy cane	✓ Mittens
✓ Christmas book	✓ Red ribbon
✓ Elf	✓ Reindeer
✓ Flashing lights	✓ Santa Claus
✓ Gingerbread man	✓ Snowflake
✓ Holiday card from another state	✓ Snow globe
✓ Holly	✓ Snowman
✓ Jingle bell	

A SCAVENGER HUNT REALLY SHAKES THINGS UP!

P.S. Out on an errand with your family? Use this list to hunt around a store or your town. You can also pick one item and count how many you see. We're willing to bet you'll easily find a dozen jingle bells and double that many Santa Clauses.

7 · Learn to say "Merry Christmas" in another language.

Here are 10 to get you started:

- **Amharic (national language of Ethiopia):** *Melkam Gena* [mel-kahm gu-nah]

- **Edo (spoken in Southern Nigeria):** *Iselogbe* [eyes-a-log-be]

- **French:** *Joyeux Noël* [zhwa-yeu noh-el]

- **German:** *Frohe Weihnachten* [fro-eh vine-act-en]

- **Greek:** *Kala Christouyenna* [ka-la he-stu-ya-na]

- **Hawaiian:** *Mele Kalikimaka* [me-le ka-li-ki'ma-ka]

- **Italian:** *Buon Natale* [bwon na-ta-lay]

- **Japanese:** *Meri Kurisumasu* [may-ri ku-ris-su-ma-su]

- **Norwegian (and Swedish):** *God Jul* [god yule]

- **Spanish:** *Feliz Navidad* [feh-leese na-vee-dad]

8

Go all in with marshmallows!

Host the world's smallest snowball fight, with mini-marshmallows as your arsenal.

While you have all those little white puffs on hand, microwave a few on a plate for 10 to 20 seconds, and get ready for a big surprise. Marshmallows are made of sugar, water, and air. When trapped in a hot, contained space (like the microwave), the sugar softens and the air bubbles expand, causing the marshmallows to grow 4 to 5 times in size.

With those marshmallows nice and warm, after you take them from the microwave (let them cool down and deflate before you remove them), you might as well pair them with chocolate bars and graham crackers for yummy s'mores.

9

Make a holiday playlist.

Use your family's preferred music streaming service to create a playlist of your favorite Christmas tunes. Play it during holiday gatherings and activities (like cookie baking) to add to the festive atmosphere.

10 Decorate your room for Christmas.

Try one or all of these easy ways to deck those bedroom walls:

- Hang a wreath on your door. Turn to page 74 to find out how to make your own.

- Create a triangle tree. Use ribbon or washi tape to make the outline of a large Christmas-tree-shaped triangle on a wall. Then fill it with any decorations you like—paper cut into geometric shapes for ornaments, festive pictures, or even LED twinkle lights—all of which you can attach to the wall using washi tape.

- Craft a ribbon garland. Use mini clothespins to clip small ornaments to a length of ribbon. String it across your headboard or window.

11 Spread some holiday cheer.

Schedule a video call with someone special who you won't see in person this holiday season. Even better, turn it into a virtual caroling session, and sing a few Christmas tunes for Aunt Sarah or Grandpa Ben. You can find free music and lyrics on YouTube to do a karaoke-style sing-along if you want musical accompaniment.

12 Build a fidget-busting Frosty.

Turn a balloon into a satisfyingly squishy faux man. Starting with a standard-size **white balloon**, use a funnel to fill the balloon with **rice** (about ¼ cup). Securely tie the top, then draw on a snowman face with **markers**.

13 **Create your own Nativity scene.**

Gather stuffed animals, action figures, holiday ornaments, and decor to pull together your own version of the Christmas story. It's a great way to share the tradition with a younger sibling or cousin.

14 **Change your tune!**

Rewrite the words to a holiday song—make it as silly as you like—and sing it for family members.

15 Craft a gift for a loved one.

For plenty of present-worthy projects, check out the crafts starting on page 61. Or bake them something sweet using one of the cookie recipes (starting on page 112).

16 Watch The Nutcracker.

The famous ballet tells the story of a young girl who befriends a nutcracker that comes to life on Christmas Eve. Since its debut in 1892 in St. Petersburg, Russia, the holiday classic has been reimagined with numerous musical styles, including hip-hop and jazz. Visit nutcrackerballet.net, which has listings for live performances across the country, or find a recording on your favorite streaming service.

17   Take a road trip.

Well, at least around the block. Put on your pj's and have your family pile in the car for a cruise through the neighborhood in search of merry holiday light displays. (Pro tip: This is the perfect time to crank up your holiday playlist—see number 9.)

18   Make a paper-chain garland.

Cut **paper** into long, rectangular 1-inch strips. Use as many colors of paper as you'd like, but make sure the strips are the same size. Secure the ends of one paper strip together, using **tape**, **glue**, **or a stapler**. Once you've completed this first link, add another strip of paper through the center of the loop, and secure that link. Repeat as many times as you'd like.

19 Take five!

Have everyone in your house select five items—toys, books, articles of clothing, you name it—and take them to a shelter or donation center.

20 Re-create a scene from a favorite holiday story.

Scour your house for costumes, and cast your friends and family—and yourself—to act out a sweet or funny moment from a Christmas classic. Don't forget pets! Your dog would make a wonderful Rudolph, don't you think?

21 Turn ho-ho-ho into ha-ha-ha.

Learn a new joke, and leave everyone in your house—or at a party—a little jollier. Try one of these Christmas-themed knee-slappers, or make up your own.

What do you call Santa if he gets too close to the fire in the chimney?

Crisp Kringle

What did Rudolph say when he found out it would be raining on Christmas Eve?

Sleigh it ain't so!

Why was the little boy afraid to tie his shoes during the holidays?

He didn't want to end up on the knotty list.

SANTA COMING DOWN the CHIMNEY!

22 Play holiday charades.

When you act out Christmas activities without saying a word, laughter is sure to ensue!

To play: Divide players into two teams. Give each team eight blank slips of paper. Have them write holiday-themed activities on every slip—hanging Christmas lights, wrapping presents, building a snowman, Santa coming down the chimney. Then ask the teams to put their slips into separate bowls and exchange them. A player on Team A will draw one slip from Team B's bowl and have 60 seconds to act out the phrase for their team. If their team guesses right before 60 seconds is up, Team A gets a point. When time is up, repeat for Team B. The winning team is the one with the most points when all eight slips have been drawn.

Try a (holiday!) three-marker challenge.

To attempt this festive art feat, you'll need a holiday-themed **coloring page or blank sheet of paper** and an assortment of **markers**. (You can also use colored pencils or crayons.) Place all the markers in a pile, then close your eyes and pick three from the group. No peeking! This trio of markers is what you have to create or color your holiday picture. Set a timer for 15 minutes, and see what masterpiece you can create with your quirky color mix.

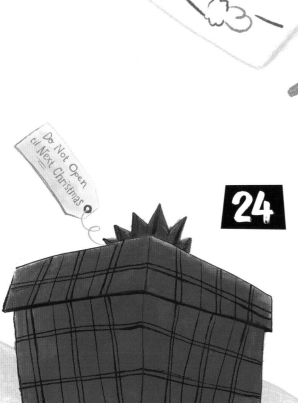

24 Create a Christmas time capsule.

Ask each family member to share a favorite moment from this holiday season. Write their answers on a notecard, and wrap those cards in a box to be opened next year. It will be a special way to start next year's festivities.

Psst: You can always add to your time capsule on Christmas Day.

Oh, Christmas Tree!

Decorating the Christmas tree is a beloved yearly tradition. But why do we put trees inside? It does seem kind of odd. Let's find out!

THE CHRISTMAS TREE
A Branch-by-Branch
Timeline

400 CE Ancient Romans decorated their homes with evergreen boughs at wintertime. They believed the trees brought good luck. (They were lucky enough to stay green throughout winter, after all.)

1500 Germans put their own spin on the Roman practice and brought full evergreen trees indoors. Most of these trees were small enough to sit on a table. The trees also became linked to Christmas, rather than merely wintertime celebrations. The idea soon spread across Europe.

1510 The first decorated Christmas tree was on display in Riga, Latvia—with no ornaments. It is believed to have been adorned with berries and fruit.

1800 The concept of the Christmas tree was introduced in the United States by German settlers. The displays quickly grew from tabletop trees to floor-to-ceiling displays.

1848 Queen Victoria and Prince Albert of England popularized the Christmas tree tradition as we know it when a sketch ran in the *London News* of the couple decorating a tree with glass ornaments and garlands. Eager to be like the stylish royals, families throughout the United Kingdom and beyond began copying the look.

1851 Inspired by the Victoria and Albert Christmas tree mania, U.S. farmers started growing evergreens to sell, primarily firs, pines, and spruces. Previously, to get a Christmas tree you had to chop one down yourself.

1856 Franklin Pierce was the first U.S. president to place a Christmas tree in the White House.

1880 A German company debuted the first artificial Christmas tree made from goose down feathers, which were dyed green and secured to wire branches. Over the next century, there will be short-lived attempts to produce fake trees using other misguided materials, including aluminum and toilet bowl brushes.

1923 President Calvin Coolidge expanded on the White House tree tradition by erecting a 48-foot balsam fir from Vermont on the front lawn. He also hosted the first National Tree Lighting Ceremony, a tradition that continues today.

1931 Construction workers erected the first Christmas tree at the not-yet-complete Rockefeller Center in New York City. The idea stuck and became a *big* deal. In 2022, the tree was a staggering 82 feet tall and 50 feet wide and weighed 14 tons.

1956 In the TV special *A Charlie Brown Christmas*, Charlie selected a scraggly pine for the holidays. Today, trees with limited branches and lots of heart are often called "Charlie Brown Christmas trees."

1980 Manufacturers finally get artificial trees right: PVC plastic "needles" are a close match for real ones. Sales of artificial trees surge.

2004 The National Christmas Tree Association debuts the free online video game "Attack of the Mutant Artificial Trees." Players attempt to pelt bah-humbugging fake trees with snowballs as the pop up from a grid of boxes, similar to the arcade favorite Whac-a-Mole.

2012 A National Christmas Tree Association survey found that 10.9 million artificial and 24.5 million farm-grown Christmas trees were purchased in the U.S. that year.

Not (Purely) Ornamental

Ornaments aren't just for show. Here are the traditions and meanings behind some of the most common Christmas tree decorations.

Bells For centuries, the ringing of church bells has marked the start of a service, especially on Christmas Eve. In the late 1800s, holiday carolers would carry small hand bells to accompany their singing. During that time the song "Jingle Bells" was written, furthering the tradition of *ringing* in the season.

Candles One of the oldest-known uses of candles at Christmas is from the Middle Ages, where a large candle was used to represent the Star of Bethlehem at church services. In the 1800s, families would clip candleholders to their trees and light the tapers on Christmas Eve. Advancements in technology eventually gave way to plug-in strands of lights—a lovely way to illuminate a tree without the fire hazard.

Gingerbread Men Baking with ginger has deep winter roots. (See "Gingerbread Headquarters," page 136, for more on that history.) But the practice of shaping them into little men has been linked to England's Queen Elizabeth I. Scholars say she originated the idea when she asked her pastry chef to craft gingerbread cookies that looked like members of her royal court.

Snowmen In the Middle Ages (around 500 to 1400–1500 CE), residents of northern Europe built snowmen as a winter pastime. But the Christmas connection didn't come about until 1969, when *Frosty the Snowman* debuted. Though a song of the same name had been a hit since 1950, it didn't reference Christmas. The animated TV special had a holiday-focused plot and a revised last line to the tune: "But he waved goodbye, saying, 'Don't you cry. I'll be back on Christmas Day.'"

Stars The connection between stars and Christmas is simple. They were originally used as decorations to pay tribute to the Star of Bethlehem, which is said to have guided the wise men to the birthplace of Jesus.

Wrapped Presents The custom of giving gifts at the holidays is to remind us of the presents brought to Jesus by the Wise Men. The pretty packages we associate with Christmastime are the doing of two brothers at a stationery store in Kansas City, Missouri. During the 1917 holiday season, they ran out of the boxes shoppers used for gift giving and began printing large rolls of patterned paper. Ta-da! Wrapping paper was invented.

Let's Talk Traditions
What's the oldest ornament on your tree? Where did it come from? What's the newest ornament on your tree? What's its story?

41

Let's Talk Traditions

Do you play "Guess the Present"? That's where you shake the wrapped parcels that appear under your tree and try to figure out what it is. If so, have you ever guessed right?

The More the Merrier

Sure, the Christmas tree is usually the largest holiday decoration in a house, but it's more than its mere presence that draws us in and brings us together. Here are some of our most beloved tree-related traditions.

Where do you get your Christmas tree? There are nearly as many ways to obtain a Christmas tree as there are styles for decorating. In a large city like New York or Chicago, you might walk down the street and buy one from a pop-up tree lot. In other areas, families may head to a Christmas tree farm. Still others may merely head to the attic to pull out their faithful and festive artificial tree.

How do you string your lights? This heavily debated topic may never get settled. Some families start at the top, while others begin at the bottom, when they encircle their tree in lights. Still others have the enlightened method of zigzagging side to side. Let's not forget those who take the time to wrap each branch! Speaking of lights, does your tree have white or multicolored bulbs?

Who gets to hang the first ornament on the tree? Plenty of families bestow this honor to the youngest or oldest member. Some draw numbers and go in order until each ornament has been hung. Others prefer the spontaneity of grabbing what they can.

What goes at the top of your tree? In the United States, stars and angels are the most common tree toppers. Both are said to have appeared the evening Jesus was born, so placing them at the top of the tree is a fitting tribute. Less traditional options include oversized bows, paper flowers, and cutouts of family initials. The sky—or at least the tree—is the limit!

Do you have a Baby's First Christmas ornament? In the 1890s, Woolworth's five-and-dime began selling glass ornaments in the United States. The popularity led the store, and others like it, to promote ornament sales. The concept of the Baby's First Christmas ornament was born, so to speak. Today they're a special milestone and keepsake for many families.

Who opens the first present? On Christmas Day, is your house a free-for-all of gift opening? Or do you have a system for who gets the honor of opening the first present? Some families have the quirky tradition of hunting for the Christmas Pickle. Tucked among the tree's branches is a lone pickle ornament. Whoever spots it first gets to begin the unwrapping. Some say the pickle is a tribute to the time Santa saved two boys who were trapped in a pickle barrel. Others think it's tied to a Civil War soldier in Georgia who begged for and was given a pickle.

Gather 'Round the Tree Book Club

Is there anywhere cozier to read a Christmas story than around the tree? Definitely not. How many of these holiday classics are in your library?

✓ **The Best Christmas Pageant Ever by Barbara Robinson**
The Herdman siblings are always on the verge of the naughty list, but they manage to win hearts when they bring their shenanigans to a town's annual holiday celebration.

✓ **A Boy Called Christmas by Matt Haig**
A young boy travels to the North Pole on a quest to save his father, only to get mixed up in the mayhem of the elves of Elfhelm along the way.

✓ **A Christmas Carol by Charles Dickens**
Notorious bah-humbugger Ebenezer Scrooge is visited by three ghosts who help him find his Christmas cheer in this famous holiday tale. Available in numerous illustrated and abridged versions, you're sure to find one that's right for you.

✓ **The Legend of the Poinsettia by Tomie dePaola**
With the help of charming illustrations, this book tells how the poinsettia came to be associated with Christmas in Mexico—and beyond.

✓ **The Life and Adventures of Santa Claus by L. Frank Baum**
The author is known for writing *The Wizard of Oz*, but he also took a crack at a very different origin story: Santa Claus.

✓ **The Real Santa by Nancy Redd**
Who can't relate to the main character in this picture book? He wants to stay up late to see what Santa looks like. After all, there are plenty of Santa decorations around his house, and they all look a little different, so which one is right?

✓ **The Tailor of Gloucester by Beatrix Potter**
This story starts out rough, with a tailor who's trying to survive a brutal winter. He gets an important Christmas Day assignment—and some help from a few furry creatures.

✓ **A Visit From St. Nicholas by Clement Clarke Moore**
Better known by its first line, "'Twas the Night Before Christmas," this 1864 poem is the gold standard for holiday reading.

Let's Talk Traditions
Does your family have a favorite holiday read—one that Christmas wouldn't be complete without reading together? Does just one person read? Or do you all take turns? Does anyone do funny voices? Or act out favorite parts?

BRANCHING Out

Move over spruces and firs because these Christmas trees dare to be different.

The Lobster Trap Tree

The seaside town of Gloucester, Massachusetts, is home to a 45-foot-tall "tree" made from over 350 lobster traps. It's decorated with hundreds of wooden buoys painted by children.

The Floating Tree

Rio de Janeiro is the frequent home of a massive floating tree that soars more than 270 feet high. Made from metal framework, the Brazilian spectacle is constructed on a barge illuminated with about three million lights.

The Sand Tree

What Florida lacks in snow it makes up for in sand, so West Palm Beach residents build a 700-ton tree-shaped sand sculpture. While the design changes from year to year, the display is always nicknamed "Sandi."

The Tumbleweed Tree

Since 1957, the town of Chandler, Arizona, has featured a tree made from tumbleweed. (You know, those balls of dried foliage that roll around Wild West ghost towns in the movies.) Hundreds are assembled in the shape of a tree, painted white, and then covered in twinkle lights.

The Mountain Tree

OK, this isn't one tree. It's hundreds. In Gubbio, Italy, individual trees on the slopes of Mount Ingino are blanketed with thousands of lights to give the illusion of a 2,400-foot Christmas tree spanning the mountain from base to peak. Each year it's lit by a notable figure. Past participants include the pope and an astronaut who sent a signal from the International Space Station.

the
SPIRIT
of
SANTA

The love and generosity
of the man in red is at the
heart of the holidays.

Who Is Santa Claus?

St. Nick, Papa Noel, Father Christmas, Kriss Kringle—Santa goes by many names. But the very first one might have been simply Nicholas.

Legend has it that Nicholas was born in what was then Greece (Turkey today) around the year 280 CE. Some say that he became a Christian monk; others believe he was a bishop in the Orthodox church. But all the tales agree on one thing: Nicholas was known for his kindness—especially to kids.

According to legend, Nicholas performed astonishing miracles and became known as Nicholas the Wonderworker. He saved sailors from an awful storm at sea and even brought three boys who had died back to life. He was also legendary for giving gifts and money to those in need. It is not clear when he was made a saint. As St. Nicholas he is the patron saint and protector of children and sailors—but also of students, archers, candlemakers, teachers, and even haberdashers (makers of men's clothing).

Around 1,000 years ago, St. Nick decided to perform one ginormous miracle each year: bringing joy to all at Christmastime. Pictures and stories of Santa (as he was now being called) delivering gifts around the world started to pop up in the 13th century.

Today, Santa and his longtime wife, Mrs. Claus, reside in the North Pole, a land as far away as it is freezing. They probably moved there from Greece in the mid-1800s—that's when drawings of Santa started to feature his trademark red, fur-trimmed jacket and pants, broad black belt, and festive stocking cap—alongside his team of reindeer. Their names were confirmed in the circa 1823 poem "'Twas, the Night Before Christmas"—Dasher, Dancer, Prancer, Vixen, Comet, Cupid, Donner, and Blitzen. (Rudolph didn't make the team until 1939, when his unusual bright nose saved the evening!)

As every kid knows, on Christmas Eve Santa travels across countries, in and out of towns, and up and down chimneys, delivering gifts to every home he visits. What does Santa ask for in return? Nothing. But he always enjoys a plateful of cookies and a refreshing glass of milk.

St. Nick by the Numbers

2
Number of times he checks his naughty and nice lists

31
Hours it takes to deliver presents around the world

650
Miles per second Santa is believed to travel. Tired much, Rudolph?

8 MILLION
Number of letters (ahem, wish lists) he receives each year from children around the world

7.6 BILLION
Number of presents Kriss Kringle hands out. Sure, this includes stocking stuffers, but that's a lot of children on the nice list.

WRITE A LETTER TO SANTA

Use this example as a guide to pen your own message. After all, this may be your best shot at getting your requests to Father Christmas.

There are a lot of letters piling into the North Pole, so using both your first and last names can't hurt.

Be honest—Santa will appreciate it!

Stick to 3 to 5 present requests so he knows what's a priority.

It's always nice to close with a compliment.

Make sure he knows there's something in it for him too!

Or you can just say Dear Santa—he's not a terribly formal guy!

DEAR MR. SANTA CLAUS,

MY NAME IS HOLLY DAY. I'M FROM THE GREAT TOWN OF CHRIS MOOSE CITY. THIS YEAR I'VE BEEN PRETTY GOOD. FOR CHRISTMAS, I'D LIKE A SCOOTER, A CAMERA, AND A NEW ART SET.

THANK YOU FOR ALL THE HARD WORK YOU DO. I'LL BE SETTING OUT CHOCOLATE CHIP COOKIES AND MILK IN YOUR FAVORITE MUG.

MERRILY YOURS,
HOLLY

Worried your letter may not make it to the North Pole?

Fear not! The towns of North Pole, New York; North Pole, Alaska; and Santa Claus, Indiana, all have hundreds of "elves"—residents who volunteer each holiday season—to make sure Santa gets his messages. Did you know there are many holiday-named cities across the United States? There's Christmas, Florida; Mistletoe, Kentucky; Christmas Cove, Maine; and Noel, Missouri, to name a few others.

Speaking of letters, did you know the best-known Santa letter wasn't sent to the North Pole but to a New York newspaper? In 1897, 8-year-old Virginia O'Hanlon wrote a letter to the editor of *The Sun*, asking if Santa Claus was real. The published response proclaimed, "Yes, VIRGINIA, there is a Santa Claus. He exists as certainly as love and generosity and devotion exist." It is the most reprinted newspaper editorial ever.

DON'T FORGET the Reindeer

We all know Santa counts on milk and cookies to refuel throughout the night. (For perfect sugary treats to leave him, pick a recipe from "Cookie Magic" starting on page 112.) But want about his fleet of flying reindeer? We have on good authority these snacks are approved by Dasher, Dancer, and the rest of the gang.

Mosses, Herbs, and Ferns
A favorite of ordinary reindeer, as well as the magical variety that hails from the North Pole.

Glitter and Oats
The oats are an excellent energy source, while the glitter glistens in the moonlight and helps the reindeer find your home. Put a small amount of the mix in a bowl in your front yard to guide the reindeer on in.

Carrots and Brown Sugar
The orange veggie may be the most common Christmas Eve treat for Santa's reindeer. Word is they like it even more when there's a bit of brown sugar sprinkled on top.

Track Santa

Wonder no more about Santa's whereabouts on Christmas Eve. The North American Aerospace Defense Command, better known as NORAD, is a combined U.S. and Canadian organization that tracks everything that flies in or around the two countries—including Santa Claus. Every year since 1958, NORAD has charted Santa's progress around the globe. You can follow along on Christmas Eve by visiting noradsanta.org.

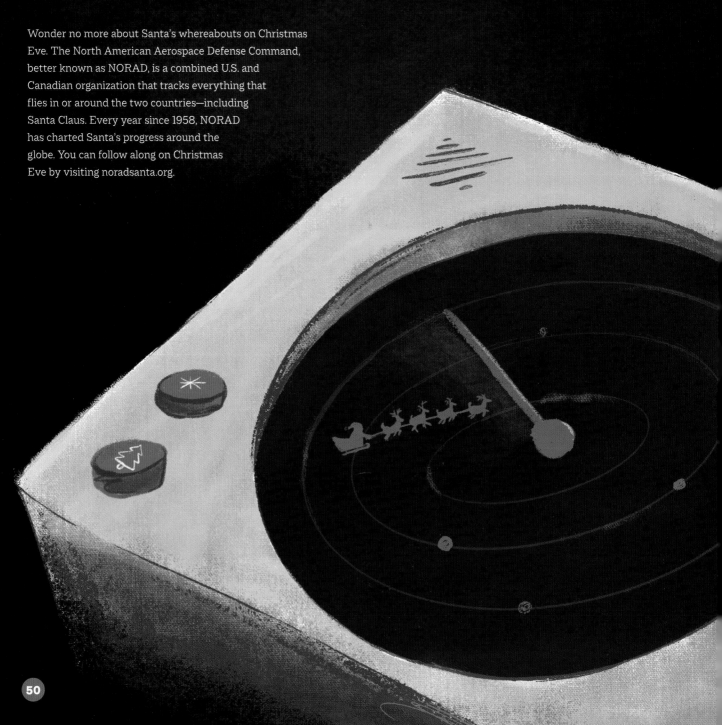

Host a Santa-Inspired Gift Swap

These spirited games ensure everyone gets a gift and a good time.

Secret Santa

Have your family or friends write their names on slips of paper, and put them into a container (like a stocking or a Santa hat). Then ask each person to draw a name—that's the person you're giving a gift to. But keep it a secret! If you pick your own name, draw again. Decide a limit on what everyone will spend on a gift—for example, $10. Invite everyone to your house for the reveal.

Swiping Santa

In this game, which goes by plenty of other of names—including White Elephant, Yankee Swap, Machiavellian Christmas, and the Grinch Games—the stakes are raised from the simple Secret Santa. Rather than bringing a gift for a particular person, participants compete for the best present. Here's how to play:

1 Each player brings one wrapped gift to contribute to a common pool.

2 Players draw numbers to determine what order they'll go.

3 Players sit in a circle or a line, so they can see the gift pile.

4 The first player selects a gift from the pool and opens it.

5 The following players can pick an unwrapped gift from the pool or swipe a previous player's gift. Anyone who gets their gift taken can choose a new gift or steal from someone else.

Two important notes on swiping:

- A present can be stolen only once per turn, which means players who have a gift stolen from them have to wait to get it back.

- After three swipes, the turn automatically comes to an end (otherwise, things could drag on for a long time).

6 After all players have had a turn, the first player gets a chance to swap the gift they're holding for any other opened gift. Anyone whose gift is stolen may steal from someone else (as long as that person hasn't been stolen from). When someone declines to steal a gift, the game ends.

FIND YOUR
Inner Santa

Spread love and kindness in the spirit of Santa Claus with one of these do-good and give-back acts.

Bake a treat (see the cookie recipes starting on page 112), and take it to the police station or fire department.

Donate used books to a Little Free Library (maybe one from the reading list on page 44). You can find one of the organization's libraries in your area by viewing their map at littlefreelibrary.org.

Say "thank you" to a teacher, past or present. Make them a handmade card (see page 90), or write a letter and share something you enjoyed learning from them (see page 186 for how to write a thank-you note).

Leave a snack—like an energy drink or a treat (see page 163 for how to make tasty puppy chow)—for postal carriers and delivery workers. (Note: Government employees, like those at the U.S. Postal Service, can accept gifts only if they're valued at $20 or less.)

Choose a toy (or a few) to donate. Another kid might enjoy a toy sitting in the back of your closet or the bottom of your toy bin, and you'll make room for new gifts from Santa.

Get tails wagging with treats for Fido, Rover, and the rest of the dog park gang. Bring enough to share with all the pups, but ask their owners before you hand them out.

Help a sibling with a dreaded task or chore. (It will go quicker if you do it together.)

Compliment a friend. You may be surprised how much they appreciate it.

Show your appreciation for members of our Armed Forces. Make a Christmas card (see page 90), and send it to Support Our Troops, who will forward it on to a Sailor, a Marine, or an Airman. For more details, visit supportourtroops.org

Make care kits. Fill resealable plastic bags with socks, gloves, a toothbrush and toothpaste, and single-serving shelf-stable snacks. Keep them in your family's car, and (with an adult) distribute them to individuals you encounter in your travels who seem like they could use a helping hand.

Merry, merry Mall Santas

The Santa you've met and posed for photos with may or may not be the real deal. Sometimes, the Big Guy brings in other big guys to put on red suits and white beards (some real, some fake) each holiday to help him complete his tremendous holiday tasks, like taking toy orders and spreading holiday cheer worldwide.

Like the trim on Father Christmas's hat, where these seasonal substitutes started stepping in to support Santa is a bit fuzzy. Boston, Philadelphia, and New York all claim to have had the first shopping center Santa in the late 1800s. Alas, only the real Santa could settle that dispute. Less fuzzy is the start of picture taking with St. Nick. In 1943, Frederick and Nelson, a store in Seattle, took photos at their Santa meet-and-greet—and in a flash, a new tradition was born.

Today thousands of jolly helpers pop up in stores for Christmastime. Many of them hone their skills at acclaimed academies around the world, such as the International University of Santa Claus, the Ministry of Fun Santa School, and the Worldwide Santa Claus Network. (After all, the North Pole is a little far to go for school.)

Tinsel Town

Hope. Joy. Love. These good feelings put Christmas movies in a league of their own. Here's how to make your movie viewing as delightful as the scenes on the screen.

B·I·N·G·O

HOLIDAY MOVIE EDITION

GINGERBREAD HOUSE		ELVES	ANGEL	FIREPLACE
CAROLING	PRESENTS	CHRISTMAS LIGHTS		HOLLY
CHRISTMAS COOKIES			SLEIGH	
REINDEER	SNOW	EGG NOG	SANTA	CHRISTMAS TREE
STOCKING	UGLY CHRISTMAS SWEATER	PEPPERMI	CHRIS	

Set the Scene

Sign Up for Fun!
Draw your own movie poster and create a fun theater-like atmosphere by announcing the film you and your family will be screening.

Lay the Groundwork.
Set out piles of plush pillows and warm blankets for snuggling up for a movie-binging marathon.

Dress to Impress.
Comfy socks and festive pajamas are highly encouraged.

Host an Intermission.
Take a page from the golden era of Hollywood, and break up your movie viewing with an old-fashioned intermission. Take 10 minutes to refill snacks, lead everyone in singing carols, or play a quick round of holiday charades (see "Choose Your Own Advent-ure," starting on page 22, for the how-to).

12 Days of Christmas Movie Marathon

Let's Talk Traditions
Pretend it's your job to start your family's new tradition of a holiday movie marathon. What films would make your binge list?

These films are filled with the ultimate holiday movie magic. Can't decide which one to watch first? Assign each movie a number, and roll dice to pick. You'll have a winner no matter the number.

✓ **A Charlie Brown Christmas**
Even if you've never had the Christmas blues, you can probably relate to Charlie Brown's it's-just-not-my-day feelings. His beagle, Snoopy, and the rest of the *Peanuts* gang help him find the spirit to keep going.

✓ **A Christmas Story**
Ralphie Parker is on a mission to convince everyone—his parents, his teacher, Santa Claus, and anyone who will listen—that he should get the gift at the top of his Christmas list. (The pink bunny pajamas he receives are not an adequate substitute.)

✓ **Elf**
Meet Buddy, the 6-foot-2-inch elf on a mission to find his real dad and spread Christmas cheer in New York City. Warning: this film will cause frequent laughter.

✓ **Home Alone**
This 1990 classic follows 8-year-old Kevin McCallister, a boy mistakenly left behind while his family flies to Europe for Christmas. With two burglars on the loose, Kevin takes matters into his own hands.

How the Grinch Stole Christmas

There are multiple movies about Dr. Suess's three-decker toadstool-and-sauerkraut-sandwich-eating villain, but the 1960s special featuring the iconic tune "You're a Mean One, Mr. Grinch" takes the Who Pudding. (In other words, it's the best.) For a few Grinch-inspired snacks to eat while you're watching, see page 163.

Jingle-Jangle: A Christmas Journey

When a former apprentice steals her granddad's prized creation, a toy maker's inventive granddaughter goes on an adventure to get it back.

Miracle on 34th Street

With Santa Claus in jail, it's up to Susan, her mom, and their friendly neighbor lawyer to prove Kriss Kringle really is Father Christmas. If you doubt Santa, this classic film from 1947 will put those questions to rest and urge even the toughest skeptics to believe. A 1994 version has equally spirit-elevating results.

The Muppet Christmas Carol

There are more than 30 film versions of Charles Dickens's classic *A Christmas Carol.* The Muppet adaptation pairs the story with kooky comedy antics. Plus, it's hard to not love Kermit the Frog as Bob Cratchit.

The Polar Express

A young boy wakes up on Christmas Eve to find a train waiting to take him to the North Pole. The entrancing animation will make you feel transported too.

Rudolph the Red-Nosed Reindeer

Rudolph and his glowing nose team up with a group of misfit toys to save Christmas—and learn about the importance of accepting differences in the process.

The Santa Clause

Everybody knows Santa is an all-powerful being, but nobody thinks about what it really takes to do his job. This movie, about a divorced dad who must unexpectedly become the next Santa, reveals the inner workings of the North Pole.

White Christmas

The tale of a holiday show at a snow-covered Vermont inn is one of the most beautiful Christmas movies in existence. (The frilly costumes are out of this world!) Even better, the song "White Christmas," which the movie takes its name from, is the best-selling holiday single of all time. After you watch it, you'll be in the mood to do some caroling yourself.

TURN IT INTO
a Game

These activities will put some mingle in your jingle movie marathon. If you want to award the winner a prize, let them select the next Christmas movie you watch. Sweeten the deal with a special treat, like a bag of the "Deck the Halls Holly Bark" on page 161. You can top the prize with a cheeky tag "Your skills are something to bark about!"

Holiday I Spy Come up with three—or more—actions to do when you see a particular Christmas movie element. For example, if...

• You see a reindeer, touch your nose.

• You see snowflakes, pat your head.

• You see a decorated Christmas tree, jump up and down.

Or pick your own fun combinations! The first player to complete an action gets a point; the person with the most points at the end of the movie wins. (By the way, you can also extend the game to include elements you hear, like "Ho, Ho, Ho" or "Merry Christmas.")

Christmas Bingo Print a blank bingo card for each movie viewer. Then have every person fill in the squares with Christmas themes and actions they think will be in the movie. Here's a list to get you started:

• Reindeer	• Presents
• Holiday lights	• Elves
• Cookies	• Holly
• Sleigh	• Santa hat
• Wrapping paper	• Snowman

If an item appears on the screen, the viewer can mark off that square on their card. The first viewer to get five in a row and call "bingo" is the winner.

Sing & String Gather an assortment of candies and cereals with a hole in the center (such as gummy and mint Life Savers, rainbow Twizzlers cut into small pieces, and Froot Loops.) For even more holiday flair, use only the red, green, and white pieces. Then give each movie viewer a length of ribbon knotted on one end. Every time you hear a Christmas song in the movie, add a candy to the string. By the end of the film, everyone will have a candy necklace.

BRING ON THE
Popcorn

It's not officially movie night without everyone's favorite theater snack. Take your pops up a notch with these delicious mix-ins.

Come and Get It!
Create your own movie theater–inspired concession stand with a serve-yourself buffet of popcorn (of course!), plus Christmasy candies such Sno-Caps and red and green M&M's or Sour Patch Kids. Other ideas with star power: soft-baked pretzels with white chocolate dipping sauce and a hot chocolate bar with marshmallows, peppermint sprinkles, and other tempting toppings.

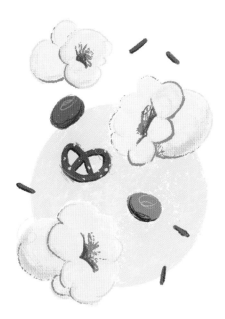

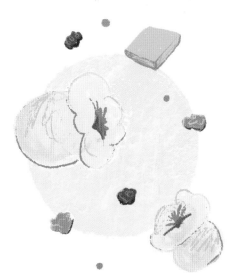

Christmas Crunch
Toss **popcorn** with 1 cup of **white cake mix**, 1 cup of **chocolate-covered candies** (such as M&M's), and red and green **sprinkles**. For even more crunch, add **mini pretzels**.

Peppermint Twist
Toss **popcorn** with 1 cup of melted **white chocolate melts**, then stir in 2 to 4 crushed **candy canes**.

(Lots of) Sugar & Spice
Toss **popcorn** with 2 tablespoons of melted **butter**, then stir in 1 teaspoon **pure vanilla extract**, 1 tablespoon **confectioners' sugar**, 1 tablespoon **granulated sugar**, 1 tablespoon **brown sugar**, 1 teaspoon **ground cinnamon**, and ½ teaspoon **ground nutmeg**.

Chapter Two
CRAFT

ORNAMENTS

Yule Love

Trim your tree with happy little homemade ornaments.

Pinecone Gnome

TIME 20 minutes

- 1 small pinecone
- Hot-glue gun and glue sticks
- 1-inch white pom-pom or white cotton ball
- Pencil
- 9-by-12-inch sheet red felt
- Fabric scissors
- Red pipe cleaner
- Red ribbon

1. First up, get your pinecone! Go on a hunt in your yard or a park (or if you need to, buy it at a crafts store). For this project, a small one will work better than a large one.

2. Glue a pom-pom or a cotton ball to the top of the pinecone. This will be your gnome's fuzzy beard.

3. To make the cap, place your pinecone on the edge of your felt, and draw a half circle around it. Cut out the half circle, then bring the two ends of the half circle together to form a cone. Glue where the edges overlap.

4. For the arms, cut the pipe cleaner in half. Twist it around the back of the pinecone body.

5. From the remaining felt, cut out tiny mittens for hands. Glue them onto the pipe cleaner ends. Cut ovals from the felt for the feet, and glue them to the bottom of the pinecone.

6. Cut about 4 inches of red ribbon. Glue each end to the top of the gnome's hat to make a loop.

Holiday Owl

TIME 1 hour, including drying

- Pencil
- ¼ yard of burlap
- Scissors
- Fabric stiffener
- Small paintbrush
- Fabric scissors
- 9-by-12-inch sheets of felt in white (eyes), red (beak), black or brown (pupils and feet), and any other colors you like (wings)
- Fabric glue
- Twine

1. Draw a large circle onto the burlap, and cut out the circle. Coat both sides with fabric stiffener, and lay flat to dry, about 45 minutes.

2. While the burlap is drying, fold the sheet of white felt in half. Draw two small half circles along the fold, and while the felt is folded, cut it out through both layers. This will give you two circles for the eyes. (You can also use fabric stiffener on the felt pieces, but they will probably be sturdy enough that you don't need to.)

3. Draw and cut a long, narrow triangle from the red felt for the beak.

4. To make the wings, fold the felt sheet in the color you've selected in half, then cut a leaf shape through both layers. This will give you two wings.

5. Cut small circles from the brown or black felt. Glue these to the center of the white felt circles to make eyes. Use the remainder of this felt to cut out two small feet. Glue the feet to the bottom of the burlap circle.

6. Use the photo below as a guide for assembling the rest of your owl: Glue the triangle beak at the top of the burlap circle, with the triangle's tip pointing toward the owl's feet and half the triangle on the burlap and half sticking off the top.

7. Glue one wing on each side of the body. Then glue one eye on each side of the beak and just over the tops of the wings. You'll want to place half on the burlap circle and half sticking off the top.

8. Cut about 6 inches of twine. Glue each end to the back of the owl to make a loop.

RIBBON CANDY ↓

CRAFT STICK SKIS ↑

BUTTON SNOWMAN ↗

STRING STARBURST ↑

FABRIC TREE →

Craft Stick Skis

TIME 45 minutes, including drying

- 2 wooden craft sticks
- Acrylic craft paint in white and any color you like
- 2 small paintbrushes
- Craft glue
- Small glue dots
- 2 toothpicks
- 2 metal snaps (size 1)
- Black permanent marker
- Baker's twine, for hanging
- Craft scissors

1   Paint one side of two wooden craft sticks. Let dry, then paint the other side.

2   After the craft sticks have dried, stick them together with a glue dot so they make a narrow X.

3   Paint two toothpicks white. Glue metal snaps to one end of each stick and let set. Color opposite ends black.

4   Cut two small pieces of twine. Use glue dots to stick one in a loop to the backside of each black end of a toothpick. Attach one pole to the top ski and the second to the center of the first with glue dots.

5   Cut about 6 inches of baker's twine, and attach one end to the back of each ski with glue dots to hang.

Ribbon Candy

TIME 1 hour, including drying

- Ruler
- Grosgrain ribbon in any color you like
- Fabric scissors
- Small paintbrush
- Fabric stiffener
- Clothespin, for drying
- Small glue dots
- String, for hanging
- 2 small plastic beads

1   Measure and cut a 24-inch piece of ribbon.

2   Use the paintbrush to cover both sides of the ribbon in fabric stiffener. Clip to a clothespin, and hang to dry.

3   Once the ribbon is dry, fold it accordion-style into loops. (Use the picture above as a guide.) Add a glue dot between each layer as you go.

4   Next, cut about 6 inches of string, and tie it to through one of the beads make a loop.

5   Attach the beads to the top and bottom of the ribbon candy with a glue dot.

Button Snowman

TIME 30 minutes

- 1 large white button (2 holes)
- 1 medium white button (2 holes)
- 1 small white button (2 holes)
- 9-by-12-inch sheet white felt
- Craft glue
- Fabric scissors
- Rickrack or ribbon scraps
- 9-by-12-inch sheet gray felt

1 Arrange the buttons on the white felt from smallest to largest to make a snowman shape. The holes of the bottom two buttons should line up vertically (like buttons); the holes of the top button should line up horizontally (like eyes). Glue the three buttons to the felt.

2 After the glue has dried, cut the snowman out of the felt, leaving a ⅛-inch border around the buttons.

3 Wrap a small piece of rickrack or ribbon around the felt and between the small and medium buttons to make a scarf.

4 Cut a small hat shape from gray felt. Stick it to the top button using a small dab of glue.

5 Finally, cut a section of ribbon. Glue each end to the back of the top button to make a loop. Let the glue dry completely.

String Starburst

TIME 30 minutes

- Pencil
- 2½-inch circle template (use a glass or search online)
- 3-inch birch slice
- Ruler
- Embroidery floss in any colors you like
- 9 small flat-head nails

1 Using a pencil and your circle template, trace a 2½-inch circle on the birch slice.

2 With the ruler, measure and mark eight evenly spaced points around the circle. Insert small nails into each point. (The birch should be soft enough to push the nails in.)

3 Tie a piece of embroidery floss around one nail, then wrap it around the others in squares or stars. After you've completed the shape, tie a second knot in the embroidery floss, and trim the excess. Repeat with additional colors and shapes until you have the look you want.

4 Add one more nail to the top of the wood slice. Tie a loop of embroidery floss to this nail.

Fabric Tree

TIME 1 hour

- Ruler
- Pencil
- Fabric scrap
- Zigzag craft scissors
- Fabric glue
- Cotton batting
- Cinnamon stick
- Sewing needle
- Embroidery thread, for hanging

1 Use a pencil and a ruler to draw two triangles on your fabric scrap. The triangles' bottoms should measure 2⅜ inches. The two tall sides should measure 4½ inches.

2 Cut out the triangles with the zigzag craft scissors.

3 Place your triangles on top of each other with the wrong sides of the fabric facing each other. Glue the long edges of the triangles closed.

4 Once glue has dried, stuff the triangles with batting.

5 Insert a cinnamon stick in the middle of the opening at the bottom of the triangle. This is your tree trunk. Glue the fabric closed around the stick, and let it dry completely.

6 Thread a needle with embroidery thread, and sew through the tip of your tree. Tie the thread together to make a loop.

Music Sheet Tassel

TIME 25 minutes

- Ruler
- Pencil
- Two-sided page of sheet music, preferably holiday carols
- Craft scissors
- ¾-inch wooden bead
- Unused wine bottle cork
- Hot-glue gun and glue sticks
- Rubber band
- Small adhesive glue dot
- String, for hanging

1. Use the ruler and pencil to draw ¼-inch-wide strips from the top (where the title is listed) to the bottom of the music sheet. Use scissors to cut out the strips.

2. Next, glue the wooden bead to the end of the wine cork. (This will help make a dome shape for the top of the tassel.)

3. Working one at a time, bend strips of paper over the bead, alternating directions to fully cover the top of the bead. Hold the strips with your hand until you've completed wrapping, then cinch the strips around the cork with the rubber band.

4. Cover the exposed rubber band with an extra strip of paper. Stick it in place with a small glue dot. Cut away excess paper if needed.

5. Curl the ends of the paper around your fingertip to fan them out.

6. Cut 6 inches of string, and loop it through the strips.

Painted Walnut

TIME 30 minutes, including drying

- 1 walnut
- 2 to 3 small wooden beads
- Acrylic craft paint in any color you like
- Small paintbrushes (one for each color of paint)
- Clear nail polish
- Hot-glue gun and glue sticks
- Craft scissors
- Baker's twine, for hanging

1. Paint the walnut and beads. (Round, bumpy items can be tricky to paint. It may take several coats to cover completely.)

2. Once the walnut and beads are dry, apply a layer of clear nail polish for a shiny finish. (Skip this step if you want a less shiny finish.)

3. Glue the beads to the top and bottom of the walnut.

4. Cut 6 inches of twine. Glue each end to the top bead to make a loop.

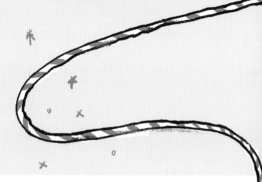

Sweater Hoop

TIME 15 minutes

- 3-inch embroidery hoop
- Old scarf or sweater
- Fabric scissors
- Fabric glue
- Ribbon, for hanging

1. Fit the inner circle of a 3-inch embroidery hoop over a section of the scarf or sweater. Cut out the section, leaving a ½-inch edge.

2. Attach the outer hoop. Fold the excess fabric over the hoop, and glue it to the back.

3. Cut a small length of ribbon, and thread through hardware at the top of the hoop to make a loop.

MUSIC
SHEET
TASSEL

PAINTED
WALNUT

SWEATER
HOOP

Happy Elf

TIME 45 minutes

- ¾-inch wooden bead
- Black permanent marker
- Red permanent marker
- Pipe cleaners
- Fabric scissors
- 2 to 3 sheets felt in any color you like
- Fabric glue
- Hot-glue gun and glue sticks
- Christmas tree ornament (a light bulb shape like the one shown will work best)

1   Draw a face on the wooden bead. Use the black marker for the eyes and the red marker for the mouth. Set the wooden bead aside.

2   Cut pipe cleaners into four pieces for the arms and legs. (You can hold them up to your ornament as a guide for how long they should be.)

3   Cut narrow strips of felt to wrap around the pipe-cleaner arms and legs. Coat one side of each strip with fabric glue, and tightly roll the strips around the pipe cleaners. Press the felt in place on the pipe cleaners as they dry to ensure a snug fit. (For a fuzzy-sweater look, skip this step on the arms and leave the pipe cleaners bare.)

4   To make the cap, place your elf's head on the edge of your felt, and draw a half circle around it. Cut out the half circle, then bring the two ends of the half circle together to form a cone. Hot glue where the edges overlap. Then use hot glue to affix the hat to the top of the elf's wooden bead head.

5   Dress up your elf! Get creative and use the additional felt to cut out small mitten and shoe shapes, and then use fabric glue to attach them to the arms and legs.

6   Attach the wooden bead to the top of the ornament with hot glue. Use a small strip of felt to make a scarf that covers the hanger portion of the ornament, and affix it in place with a dot of hot glue. Be sure to leave the fabric loose enough that an ornament hook can slip through the back.

7   Use the hot-glue gun to attach the arms and legs to the ornament body. Hang by piercing an ornament hook through the hat.

Festive Llama

TIME 45 minutes

- Pencil
- Llama-shaped cookie cutter (or any favorite animal cookie cutter)
- White card stock
- Craft scissors
- 9-by-12-inch sheet white felt
- Fabric glue
- Book (for drying)
- Black permanent marker
- White paint pen
- Fabric and ribbon scraps
- Baker's twine, for hanging

1   Trace the outline of the llama-shaped cookie cutter onto the card stock, and cut out.

2   Glue a section of the white felt to the llama cutout. Place the pieces under a book while drying to ensure a flat, firm hold. Cut out a small circle from the remaining white felt. This will be the snout. If you'd like, cut out a few locks of "fur" to go at the top of the head.

3   Once the glue is dry, trim around the llama shape, and remove excess felt from the card stock backing.

4   Glue the snout and fur in place, using the picture below as a guide.

5   Use the black permanent marker to draw on the eyes, nose, and mouth. Dot the eyes with a white paint pen to make pupils.

6   Use the fabric and ribbon scraps to give your llama festive accessories.

7   Cut 6 inches of twine. Glue each end to the back of the llama to make a loop.

NEED A NEW ORNAMENT? NO PROB-LLAMA!

Fluffy Santa

TIME 1 hour

- Fabric scissors
- 1 red felt square (3 by 3 inches)
- Fabric glue
- Mini white pom-pom
- Faux fur trim
- Large white pom-pom
- Mini pink pom-pom
- Wire cutter
- Silver craft wire
- Ribbon, for hanging

1. Use the scissors to cut the red felt into two triangles. Use glue to attach on two sides. Now you have a hat. Attach the mini white pom-pom to the top with the glue.

2. Cut a short strip of faux fur, and affix it around the bottom of the hat with glue. Let the glue on the hat set.

3. Use glue to attach the hat to the large white pom-pom. Then use an additional dab of glue to attach the mini pink pom-pom for the nose.

4. Use the wire cutter to snip off a roughly 3-inch section of craft wire. Then use your fingers to twist it into

mini-eyeglasses, like those shown in the photo above. (Or switch it up and glue on googly eyes.)

5. Cut a small section of ribbon. Glue each end to the back of the hat to make a loop. Let glue dry completely before hanging.

Sparkling Angel

TIME 45 minutes

- Craft scissors
- Metallic silver scrapbook paper
- Metallic gold scrapbook paper
- Black permanent marker
- Red permanent marker
- 1-inch doll-pin head
- 4¼-inch doll pin
- Hot-glue gun and glue sticks
- Silver craft wire
- Wire cutter
- String, for hanging

1. Use the scissors to cut a half circle out of metallic silver scrapbook paper, about 5 inches from the straight side to the edge. Cut a circle (about 2 inches) from the gold paper, then snip it in half to make wings.

2. Using permanent markers, draw a face on the doll-pin head, using the black marker for the eyes and the red marker for the mouth. Hot glue the doll-pin head to the doll pin.

3. Wrap the silver paper in a cone shape around the doll pin. Curl a piece of craft wire into concentric circles to make a halo, and secure at one end by wrapping the wire around itself. Hot glue the wrapped wire to the back of the head.

4. Cut 6 inches of string. Tie each end to the base of the halo to make a loop.

Cinnamon-Scented Tree

TIME 20 minutes

- Craft scissors
- 1 spring fresh rosemary
- Craft glue
- 1 cinnamon stick
- Small beads or gems
- Twine, for hanging

1   Use scissors to snip one sprig of fresh rosemary into four lengths, from short to long. Glue the sprigs of rosemary across the cinnamon stick perpendicularly. Attach small beads or gems for ornaments. Let the glue dry.

2   Cut 6 inches of twine. Tie it in a loop, and glue it to the back of the cinnamon sticks.

KNOCK KNOCK!

Elf Door

TIME 30 minutes, including drying

- Fairy door, available at crafts stores
- Red acrylic craft paint
- Small paintbrush
- Mini wreath or small twig of flexible faux evergreen
- Glue dots
- Ribbon
- Twine, for hanging

1   Paint front and back of the fairy door. Let dry completely.

2   Stick the mini wreath to the door with a glue dot. Or shape a twig of faux evergreen into a circle that fits the door. Use glue dots to stick the ends together and to stick the wreath to the door.

3   Tie a small bow in plaid ribbon, and stick it to the bottom of the wreath with a glue dot.

4   Cut 6 inches of twine. Use glue dots to attach each end to the back of the door to make a loop for hanging.

Salt Dough Stars

TIME 1 hour 15 minutes

- 2 cups flour, plus more for work surface
- 1 cup salt
- 1½ cups warm water
- Mixing bowl
- Rolling pin
- Gel food coloring (optional)
- Holiday cookie cutters
- Reusable straw
- Hot-glue gun and glue sticks
- Decorative sequins
- Ribbon, for hanging

1. In a large mixing bowl, combine flour, salt, and water. Turn dough out on a lightly floured work surface, and knead until firm and smooth. Add food coloring if desired, and knead dough until the color is evenly dispersed throughout.

2. Roll out the dough to ¼-inch thick. Use star cookie cutters or other shapes to cut desired ornament shapes. Poke a hole for hanging through the top of each using the straw.

3. Bake at 300°F until dry, about 1 hour.

4. After ornaments have completely cooled, glue on sequins. Cut 6 inches of twine for each ornament. Tie cut ribbon in a loop through the hole in each ornament.

Knit Cap

TIME 20 minutes

- Ruler
- Craft scissors
- Yarn
- Paper towel tube

1 Measure and cut fifty 14-inch lengths of yarn, plus a 1-inch ring from the paper towel tube.

2 Fold a piece of yarn in half, and pull the doubled end around the ring and back through the yarn loop, then pull to tighten it around the ring. Repeat until the ring is covered.

3 Gather the loose ends of yarn, and feed them through the ring's center.

4 Knot a length of yarn 10 inches above the ring. You can use the rest of the yarn to hang.

5 Trim the top into a pom-pom, and put a cotton ball inside the hat to keep its shape.

Holiday Hangs

Deck the doors—not just the halls.
Make a wreath for your front door, bedroom door,
and even the bathroom door.

Crayon Wreath

TIME 30 minutes

- Ruler
- Scissors
- 2 yards wired ribbon (1½ inches wide)
- 12-inch wire wreath frame
- Hot-glue gun and glue sticks
- Box of 96 crayons

1   Measure and cut 18 inches of ribbon. Loop it through the center of the wreath frame, and tie the ends together in a knot. Using the hot-glue gun, carefully glue the knot in place on the back of the frame so it will be hidden behind the finished wreath.

2   Apply glue to the underside of a crayon, and attach it to the wreath, lining up the bottom band on the paper label with the innermost section of the wreath frame. Work your way around the wreath, making sure the crayons touch in the center but spread out at the ends. To create a uniform look, make sure you lay every crayon so the words on the label face up and in the same direction.

3   Using the remaining ribbon, tie a bow (see page 86). Glue the bow to the front of the wreath.

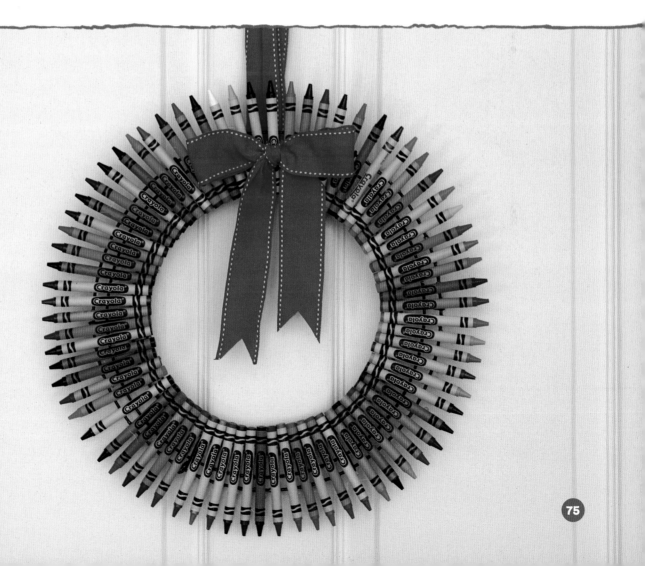

Cellophane Candy Wreath

TIME 1 hour

- Ruler
- Pencil
- Cardboard tubes (paper towel rolls, toilet paper rolls, or wrapping paper tubes will all work)
- Straight-edge craft scissors
- Tissue paper in any colors you like
- Clear cellophane
- Double-sided tape
- Baker's twine
- Scallop-edge scissors
- 12-inch embroidery hoop
- Craft glue

1 Using the ruler and a pencil, measure and mark about thirty 1½-inch sections on the cardboard tubes. Use the straight-edge scissors to cut them out.

2 Stack two pieces of the same color tissue paper, then use the scissors to cut the doubled-up sheets into 3½-by-5-inch strips.

3 Continue to use the straight-edge scissors to cut cellophane into 3½-by-5-inch strips.

4 Roll each piece of cardboard tubing in a strip of doubled-up tissue paper. Try to leave an equal amount of tissue paper on both ends of the tube.

(You can trim them up in step 5, so it doesn't have to be exact.) Secure the paper with a piece of double-sided tape.

5 Repeat step 4 with the cellophane. Tape the cellophane in the same spot you taped the tissue, so one side of the tube is free of tape.

6 Cinch the overhang of tissue paper and cellophane with a small section of baker's twine, and tie. Trim the ends of the "candies" with scalloped scissors.

7 Glue the taped sides of "candies" to the embroidery hoop, repeating until the entire hoop is covered. Let the glue dry completely.

Hang It Up!

Try this nifty trick to hang your wreath on your door.

Place an adhesive hook upside down on the backside of the door, about 12 inches from the top. Tie a 2-foot length of ribbon around the top of your wreath, lay the ribbon over the top of the door, then loop it over the hook.

Colorful Bow Wreath

TIME 30 minutes

- About 100 gift bows (pick any you like, in a variety of sizes, shapes, and colors)
- 16-inch foam craft ring
- Hot-glue gun and glue sticks

1 Attach a few of the largest bows along the top of the foam craft ring with hot glue. Make sure they're evenly spaced.

2 Fill in the top of the ring with an assortment of bows in different sizes, securing each to the ring with a dot of hot glue.

3 Once the top is filled, continue to cover the inside and outside of the ring, adding bows with hot glue until the foam ring is completely covered.

Paper Poinsettia Wreath

TIME 45 minutes

- Fabric scissors
- Holiday-patterned tea towel in any color you like
- 16-inch foam craft ring
- Large adhesive glue dots
- Craft scissors
- Red, white, and green cupcake liners
- Yellow push pins

1. Using fabric scissors, cut the tea towel in half lengthwise. Wrap the pieces snugly around the craft ring, securing them with glue dots.

2. To make poinsettia petals: Cut eight triangular slits from the outer rims to the inner folds of six red and six white cupcake liners; fold the remaining pieces in to form petals.

3. To make poinsettia leaves: Fold 12 green liners in half.

4. Stack two "flower" liners on top of two "leaf" liners to form a poinsettia. Secure the flower to the wreath by pushing three yellow pins through the flower's center into the foam ring. Repeat with the remaining petals and leaves.

Holiday Light
Wreath

Tinsel
Wreath

Sheet Music
Wreath

Christmas Ornament Wreath

Holiday Light Wreath

TIME 35 minutes

- Acrylic paint in any color you like
- 12-inch foam craft ring
- About 70 retro-inspired plastic Christmas light bulbs
- Hot-glue gun and glue sticks

1 Paint the foam craft ring—it might need a few coats. (This provides a pretty backdrop if the ring peeks through.)

2 Hot glue a layer of Christmas light bulbs to the foam ring.

3 Repeat with a second layer. Place this second batch of lights in the "joints" of the first layer.

Christmas Ornament Wreath

TIME 45 minutes

- 16-inch foam craft ring
- 5 yards ribbon in any color, to cover the wreath
- Large adhesive glue dots
- About 100 plastic Christmas tree ornaments (in a variety of sizes, shapes, and colors)
- Hot-glue gun and glue sticks

1 Wrap the craft ring with ribbon, securing it in place with glue dots as you go. (This provides a pretty backdrop if the ornaments don't cover a certain spot.)

2 Starting on the outside edge of the wreath, hot glue ornaments to the wreath. Work your way in until you have a solid base. Then fill in "holes" with one or two more layers of ornaments. (Stick to three layers max so it won't be too bulky.)

Tinsel Wreath

TIME 15 minutes

- 5 yards tinsel garland, in any color you like
- 16-inch foam craft ring
- Large adhesive glue dots
- Craft scissors
- Tinsel ornaments, to accent

1 Secure one end of the tinsel garland to the back of the foam ring with glue dots. Slowly wrap the garland tightly around the form, avoiding gaps.

2 When you get back to where you started, snip the end of the garland with the scissors, and secure it to the ring with glue dots.

3 Attach a few ornaments for extra embellishment if you'd like.

Sheet Music Wreath

TIME 1 hour

- 4 sheets of music, preferably Christmas carols
- 12-inch foam craft ring
- Clear tape

1 Cut your sheet music into 10-by-½-inch strips.

2 Tape one end of a strip of paper to the bottom of the craft ring, and wrap around the wreath. Secure the other end to the back of the ring with another piece of tape. Repeat until the entire ring form is covered.

3 Add a finishing touch to your wreath with leftover strips of paper. Make the fancy attachment shown at left by carefully using scissors to curl the strips. (Make sure your scissors are safe to use for curling, and ask an adult to demonstrate before trying it yourself.) To curl a paper strip, hold one end between your pointer finger and thumb. In your other hand, hold the scissors open and facing upward. Press the paper firmly against the blade of the scissors with your thumb. Finally, pull the paper across the scissors blade while pressing with your thumb.

Winter Wonderland

No white Christmas in your forecast? Create your own wintry mix with 3D paper snowflakes that are a cut above.

TIME 1 hour

- 9 white paper lunch bags
- Craft glue
- Snowflake template (scan the smart code below)
- Pencil
- Scissors
- Decorative ribbon or string for hanging

1 With the smooth side of a bag facing up, add glue sparingly (avoid globs) in a T shape along its bottom edge and up its length. Place the next bag on top, making sure the smooth side is also facing up and in the same direction as the first bag. Repeat until all nine bags are glued together. Let the glue dry completely.

2 Cut out the snowflake template (scan the smart code to the bottom left), and use a pencil to trace its shape on top of the stack of bags.

3 Cut the bags along their edges with scissors.

4 Glue a loop of ribbon or string at the top end of one side of the stack of bags, so you can hang your finished snowflake.

5 Finally, add glue on the end of the bag in the same T shape that you started with to close the circle. Let the glue dry completely before hanging.

Cool Points

This detailed snowflake
has precision-sharp
wow factor.

Pretty Spears

Layered points of different
lengths come together to
make this unique display.

Snowy Sunburst

For this design, you'll dot the inside
of the snowflake with little cutouts
that get bigger toward the edges.

WRAP IT UP

The thrill of getting a gift is even better when it comes in beautiful wrapping! Make the people on your gift list feel special with these wrapping tips and ideas straight from Santa's elves.

Be a Wrap Star

Master basic present wrapping with this step-by-step guide.

1 Unroll **wrapping paper**, pattern side down, on a flat surface. Place the gift in the center. Fold the cut side so it lines up with the middle of the present, then pull the end attached to the roll to the middle. Use **scissors** to cut the paper from the roll at the spot you think the two will meet. (If your paper is much larger than the gift you're wrapping, trim the paper in the other direction as well so you have a better fit before you fold and tape the paper.)

2 Fold the paper over the gift, and secure the seam in the center with **clear tape**.

3 On one end of the box, flatten the paper from both sides against the box, creating triangles above and below. Crease the triangle edges.

4 Fold the top triangle down, then lift the bottom triangle over that one, and tape it in place. Repeat steps 3 and 4 on the other end of the box.

Problem Solved!

If your wrap job doesn't go quite as planned, these helpful tricks for common issues may save the day.

Problem: **You cut the wrapping paper too small, and you don't have enough to go around the package.**
Solution: Hide the gap by cutting out a piece of wrapping paper (a little larger than the length and width of the blank spot) and taping it over the problem area.

Problem: **Your triangles (see step 3) aren't even.**
Solution: Scissors to the rescue! Simply snip the end off the longer of the two triangles so that it's about the same length as the shorter one. Remember, it's difficult to see both ends of a present at the same time, so they don't have to match up exactly.

Problem: **The present you're wrapping is too large for the paper.**
Solution: Use the wrapping paper tutorial, but wrap only one end of the box. Then wrap the other end using the same process. Cover the line where the papers meet with a ribbon. Or cut two pieces of wrapping paper about an inch longer and an inch wider than the ends of the gift box. Tape them to the box. Then wrap the paper.

Now You See It, Now You Don't!
Instead of using clear tape on top of the paper, try using double-sided tape on the underside. It will look as if you haven't used tape at all. Magic!

Take a Bow

Here's everything you need to know to tie a perfect bow.
(Your shoelaces may thank you as well.)

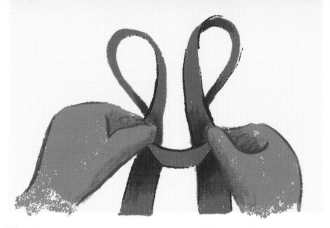

1. To make a medium bow, use about 15 inches of **ribbon** and form two loops of equal size.

2. Cross the right loop over the left loop, creating a small third loop below the first two.

3. Fold the left loop down, over the right loop and through the bottom loop.

4. Gently tug the loops, and fluff the bow until it reaches your desired look. Use **scissors** to the tails, then fold them in half and cut at an upward angle to create a V shape at both ends.

5. Use double-sided tape or an adhesive glue dot to attach the bow to your package.

Neat Little Bows
Try this method to create bows for wreaths and ornaments too.

Top It Off

For a fun handmade touch, wrap your gifts in plain brown kraft paper or brown paper from supermarket bags, and add these festive, eye-catching toppers.

Mini Candy Cane Sleds

Paper Straw Christmas Tree

Yarn Pom-Pom

Honeycomb Ornaments

Mini Candy Cane Sleds Wrap a **wooden scrap** measuring about 4 inches wide by 1½ inches tall in **colored paper**. **Hot glue** a **candy cane** to both sides of the bottom of your wrapped block, with the loops of the canes swooping up like the runners of a sled. Once the glue dries, stack one to two small packages on top. Secure the gifts to your sled by tying them with **decorative ribbon**.

> **Got more candy canes?**
> **Make the sleighs on page 94 too.**

Honeycomb Ornaments Cut 1½-inch and 2½-inch half circles from **honeycomb kraft paper**. Use **double-sided tape** to attach one side of a folded half circle to the wrapped package. Next, unfold the half circle, and tape the other side of the sphere to the box. Repeat with the other half circle. Use a **silver paint pen** to draw ornament hangers directly on the brown paper.

Paper Straw Christmas Tree Using a **pencil**, draw a triangle on the front of the wrapped package—this will be the outline for your tree. Cut **decorative paper straws** to fit horizontally within the tree outline, starting small and increasing bit by bit till you get to the largest one, which will form the base of the triangle. Using **craft glue**, stick the straws into place. Cut two 1-inch pieces of straw, and glue them vertically at the base to form a trunk. Let dry. Weave a piece of **string** down the length of the tree, and glue it into place, then glue **small buttons** on the string for ornaments.

Yarn Pom-Pom Hold four fingers of one hand together, and loosely wrap 50 loops of **yarn** around them. (Need help keeping count? Ask a friend!) Snip the end of the yarn with **scissors**, and slide the loops off your fingers, making sure they don't unravel. Cinch the loops at the middle, and tie another piece of yarn around them to secure it. Cut the ends of your loops, and fluff the strands with your fingers. Cut another strand of yarn long enough to loop around the gift a few times, and use the ends to tie on your pom-pom.

Star & Twine

Fabric Scarf

Sticker Style

Tartan Tidings

Star & Twine Cut a star out of **colored paper** with **scissors**. Place a **glue dot** in the center of the star on the back, and stick it to your gift. Then loop **baker's twine** around the box and over the top of the star a few times to secure it in place. Tie the twine in a knot at the back of the package to hide the ends.

Fabric Scarf Wrap a scrap piece of cozy winter **fabric** around a gift box to give it a scarf.

Sticker Style Use **letter stickers** to spell out holiday greetings or the recipient's name, and **label dots** in holiday colors make perfect polka dots.

Tartan Tidings Make a classic plaid pattern with two rolls of **washi tape**. Experiment with red and green (or silver, gold, or any other holiday colors), solid and striped, and different thicknesses of tape. Once you've selected your two rolls, wrap one pattern around the package widthwise, then wrap the other lengthwise, so they cross perpendicularly.

Hands-On HOLIDAY CARDS

Mistletoe

Make mistletoe with your fingers: Using a **green ink pad**, stamp your thumbs in ink, then press them onto a **card** to make leaves. Paint or draw on berries, a bow, and stems with red and green **watercolors** or a **marker**.

String Lights

Stamp your thumbs in various colors of **ink pads**, then press them onto a card. (To avoid the ink colors getting muddied, wash your thumb before switching to a different color.) Make your thumbprints anywhere, but leave some space between them. Once the ink is dry, use a **black fine-tip marker** to draw a string connecting the lights, then write a greeting on your card in your fanciest handwriting.

Merry & BRIGHT

Reindeer Heads

Stamp your thumbs and index fingers in **brown ink pads**, and press them onto a **card**, lining the fingerprints in a row. Draw a red nose on one fingerprint using a **red marker** to make Rudolph, then use a **black fine-tip marker** to draw eyes and antlers (and noses for the rest of the reindeer).

Here's a Nice Touch!
These creations are also handy for making your own thank-you cards. For a how-to on writing a holiday thank-you note, see page 186.

Tag, You're It!

These gingerbread gift tags are perfect for presents.

- Pencil
- Gingerbread man cookie cutter
- Brown card stock or thick construction paper
- Craft scissors
- Small adhesive glue dots
- Sewing scraps, such as fabric, ribbons, and buttons
- Hole punch
- String

1. Use a pencil to very lightly trace the outline of the cookie cutter onto the card stock. Cut out the shape.

2. Play dress up: Use the glue dots to attach sewing scraps to give the gingerbread man details and accessories. Make sure to leave some space to add an address to the present.

3. Punch a hole in the top of the tag. Loop a small piece of string through the gingerbread man to attach it to a gift.

Circle
Wreath

Hook
Wreath

CANDY CANE CREATIONS

Your favorite red-and-white Christmas treat is also the perfect starter for festive craft projects—if you can keep from eating all the supplies!

Hook Wreath

TIME 30 minutes

- Candy canes
- Small adhesive glue dots
- Peppermint candies
- Red ribbon

1 Arrange candy canes in a circle with the hooks all facing the same direction. Affix the ends together with adhesive dots at both the top and bottom of the candy canes. (Don't worry if the ends don't line up. These will be covered by other decorations.)

2 Cover the center of the wreath with peppermint candies, overlapping them slightly and holding in place with glue dots.

3 Loop ribbon through two candy cane hooks to hang.

Circle Wreath

TIME 1 hour

- 12-inch foam wreath form
- White ribbon
- Hot-glue gun and glue sticks
- Peppermint sticks
- Small candy canes
- Peppermint balls

1 Wrap the wreath form with white ribbon. Secure the end of the ribbon to the form with glue.

2 Starting at the inside of the wreath and working your way out, glue on the peppermint sticks, small candy canes, and peppermint balls. (Don't feel like you have to follow a pattern with your candies! The red-and-white color scheme will help it all look coordinated.)

3 Let all glue dry then loop a ribbon through the wreath to hang it.

Candy Sleighs

TIME 30 minutes

- Small white jewelry boxes (you can purchase them online)
- Thin holiday ribbon
- Craft scissors
- Double-sided tape
- Candy canes
- Glue dots
- Candy cane sticks
- Candy

1   Wrap jewelry boxes in ribbon, holding it in place with tape.

2   Attach two candy canes to the bottom of each box with glue dots. If you'd like, attach candy cane sticks to the back of the box.

3   Fill with candy.

Peppermint Stirrers and *Marshmallows*

TIME 10 minutes

- **Candy canes**
- **Semisweet chocolate (melted)**
- **Parchment paper**
- **Plate**
- **Marshmallows**

1   Dip ends of candy canes in melted semisweet chocolate.

2   Sprinkle with crushed candy canes; place on a parchment-paper-lined plate, and chill.

3   Lightly mist large marshmallows with water.

4   Sprinkle with crushed candy canes.

Candy Cane Stories

The sweets have been around for centuries.

Candy canes likely date to the 1670s, when they were all-white sugar sticks.

In the late 1600s, the upside-down J shape was added to the stick. Some say a German choirmaster bent the ends so they would look like shepherd's hooks before handing them out to the young singers he was trying to keep quiet during the Christmas service.

The white candy cane is believed to have made its U.S. debut in Wooster, Ohio, in 1847, when a German-Swedish immigrant decorated a small blue spruce with paper ornaments and the sugary treat.

The rise in mass-produced candy gave way to new takes on the all-white sugar candy cane. Red stripes and mint were added to the recipe by the turn of the 20th century,

becoming the favored style and flavor. Today 1.76 billion candy canes are produced in the United States annually, with 90 percent of them sold between Thanksgiving and Christmas.

According to a survey from the National Confectioners Association, 72 percent of respondents say that starting on the straight end is the "proper" way to eat a candy cane; the rest start at the curved end.

Melted Ornaments

TIME 20 minutes, plus cooling

- **Baking sheet**
- **Parchment paper**
- **Nonstick cooking spray**
- **Cookie cutters**
- **Mints**
- **Wooden skewer**
- **Red twine**

1 Line a baking sheet with parchment paper.

2 Grease parchment paper and insides of cookie cutters.

3 Set cutters on the baking sheet; fill with a single layer of mints in the bottom, breaking mints to fill any gaps.

4 Bake at 350°F just until melted, 5 to 6 minutes.

5 Let stand 2 minutes, then poke a small hole in top with a wooden skewer.

6 Let stand 5 minutes; carefully remove cutters.

7 Let cool completely.

8 Thread a piece of twine through the hole to hang.

Gift Wrap

- **Candy canes**
- **Ribbon**
- **Hot-glue gun and glue sticks**

1 For a large present, wrap a length of ribbon around the center of the package; secure it with tape, and attach mints with hot glue.

2 Adhere two candy canes to the package, end to end and facing in opposite directions, using hot glue.

3 Loop a ribbon around candy cane hooks, and tape the ribbon to the back of the package. Add a bow with hot glue.

4 For a small package, simply tie two small candy canes in the knot of a ribbon tied around a package.

Candy Garland

TIME 20 minutes

- Candy canes
- Small adhesive glue dots
- Red twine

1   Attach candy canes together, either in a heart shape or back-to-back, with glue dots.

2   Tie red twine around canes where they're connected.

3   Loop the candy canes over red twine, and hang.

Candy Candles

TIME 1 hour, including drying

- Candy cane sticks
- Glass candleholder
- Ribbon
- Peppermints
- Holly leaves
- Craft glue

1   Attach candy cane sticks to a glass pillar candleholder with glue. Let the glue dry completely.

2   Wrap with ribbon, and add peppermints or a mini wreath and greenery for decoration.

STOCKING UP

Whether you hang them from the mantel for Santa to fill or use them for gifts, these homemade pieces are big enough to hold plenty of treats. Hey, if the stocking fits—use it!

SCAN HERE

X Marks the Spot

To re-create the style shown here, make your stocking from a type of fabric known as **aida cloth**. Then use a **fine-tip marker** to draw a design made up of small Xs for a no-stitch cross-stitch look.

Make Your Own Stocking

Use the provided template and step-by-step instructions to craft a homemade stocking. You can glue or sew pieces together.

TIME 1 hour 30 minutes

- Stocking Template (scan the smart code)

  *To make a cuff, make your stocking 4 inches taller, and fold the top over.

- Fabric scissors
- Tape
- Pins Marker

- Fabric in any color you like (a thick fabric like felt will work best)
- Ruler
- Pencil
- Fabric glue or thread and needle
- Ribbon (for hanging)

1. Print the template, cut it out, and tape the pieces together. Pin onto your fabric, and trace and cut out two stocking shapes. Remove the pins and paper template.

TO GLUE

2. Use a ruler and a pencil to draw a 1-inch border around the entire perimeter of each stocking piece to form a hem. Neatly fold the fabric along the marked lines, then lift the fold and apply a thin layer of fabric glue under the overhang. Refold, and press fabric together to ensure a strong hold with the glue. (You can also place the fabric between two pieces of parchment paper, and place a large book over that while it dries.)

TO SEW

3. Pin the two stockings together, aligning the edges. (You may want to place the sides with your tracing marks on the inside, so they don't show.)

4. Make a knot at the end of your thread, and run the thread through the needle. Using a running stitch, place your needle between the two fabric layers, and sew through the top layer. (This will place your knot on the inside of your stocking.)

5. Place your needle about half an inch away from where it came through the top layers, and run it through both layers, connecting the two pieces of fabric. Continue to stitch evenly along the edge.

6. When the stocking pieces are sewn together with your needle in the back, make a knot, and cut the string.

TO HANG

7. Cut about 4 inches of ribbon. Glue or stitch the end together to make a loop. Then glue or stich it inside the stocking to make a hanger.

Festive Finishes

Jazz up your DIY stocking with these fun designs. You can also use these ideas to dress up a store-bought stocking!

Striking Snowflakes

Head to the scrapbook-supply aisle at a crafts store, where you can find an assortment of **3D stickers**. Use a single design, like the snowflakes at right, or a mix of holiday elements. While the stickers are sticky, adhere them to your stocking with **fabric glue** so they stay in place through this holiday and others to come.

Simple STAMPING

Revamp a stocking in minutes with a stamped-on design. Whether you work with **rubber stamps** or a homemade **potato stamp** (used to the create the circles shown), you can add bold colors and patterns in a snap. Want to personalize the stocking even more? Try letter stamps to spell out a name or message. Just be sure to stamp with **fabric paint**. It isn't as thick as other varieties, so it won't bleed through the stocking.

Heart-Felt Shapes

Anything goes when it comes to felt embellishments. Cut out any shapes you like from **felt fabric**, and attach to your stocking with **fabric glue**. For more complicated holiday designs like starbursts or snow angels, you may want to use a **cookie cutter** to trace the motif with a **pencil** before you cut it out.

Forest Friends

Create one of these woodsy critters, and use it to stockpile holiday treasures and treats.

For a cozy final touch, wrap some fabric for a scarf around your animal's neck!

TIME 2 hours

- Make Your Own Stocking (page 105)
- Deer, Owl, or Fox Template (scan the smart code)
- Scissors
- Tape
- Pins
- Marker

- Assorted fabric to make stocking and deer, fox, or owl head (a thick fabric like felt will work best; use the picture as a reference for colors)
- Scrap fabric for scarves
- Fabric glue or thread and needle
- Buttons (¾ inch for deer and owl; ½ inch for fox)

Deer

1 Make your basic stocking.

2 Print the deer template, and cut all the shapes out of corresponding felt and fabric.

3 Arrange facial features in this order: ears, antlers, cheeks, nose. Then for the eyes, layer the eyelashes behind the white eye shape, and use ¾-inch buttons for the pupils. Use fabric glue to secure all items in place.

Fox

1 Make your basic stocking.

2 Print the fox template, and cut all the shapes out of corresponding felt and fabric.

3 Glue the outer ear shapes to the back of the head. Then glue the cheeks, nose, and eyes, including ½-inch buttons for pupils.

4 Finish by attaching the belly and inner ear fabric shapes with glue.

Owl

1 Make your basic stocking.

2 Print the owl template, and cut all the shapes out of corresponding felt and fabric.

3 Glue the ears in place. Then layer the eye shapes, including ¾-inch buttons for the pupils and beak, and glue.

4 Glue the belly in place. Then crease wings, and glue to sides under cuff.

SCAN HERE

Chapter Three
BAKE

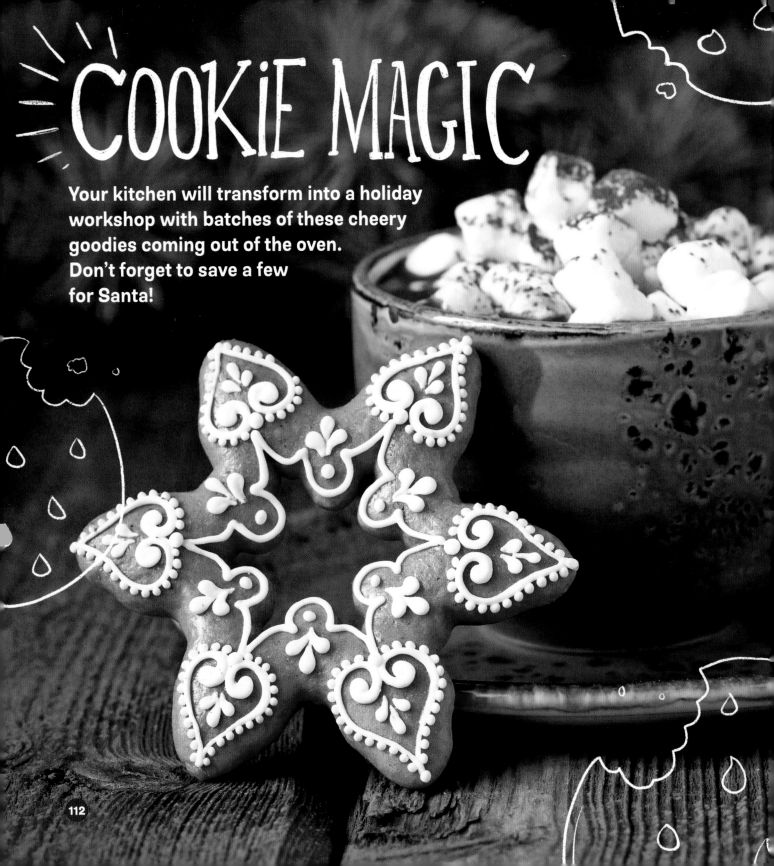

COOKIE MAGIC

Your kitchen will transform into a holiday workshop with batches of these cheery goodies coming out of the oven. Don't forget to save a few for Santa!

112

Basic Christmas Cookie Doughs

Make these three basic doughs—sugar, black cocoa, and gingerbread—your go-tos for any cookie cutouts. Sprinkles, icing, candies, and other fun toppings will transform them into fun treats.

Classic Sugar Cookie Dough

ACTIVE TIME 10 minutes
TOTAL TIME 10 minutes, plus chilling
MAKES 36 to 48 cookies (depending on size and shape)

- 2¾ cups all-purpose flour, plus more for dusting
- ½ teaspoon baking powder
- ½ teaspoon kosher salt
- 1 cup (2 sticks) unsalted butter, at room temperature
- ¾ cup sugar
- 1 large egg
- 1½ teaspoons pure vanilla extract

OTHER MATERIALS

- Measuring cups and spoons
- 2 large bowls
- Whisk
- Electric mixer
- Parchment paper
- Rolling pin
- 2 baking sheets
- Cookie cutters
- Oven mitts
- Cooling rack

1 In a large bowl, whisk together flour, baking powder, and salt; set aside.

2 Using an electric mixer, beat the butter and sugar in another large bowl on medium speed until light and fluffy, 3 minutes. Beat in the egg and then the vanilla. Reduce speed to low, and gradually add the flour mixture, mixing until just incorporated.

3 Shape the dough into three 1-inch-thick disks, and roll each between two sheets of parchment paper to ⅛ to ¼ inch thick. Chill until firm, 30 minutes in the refrigerator or 15 minutes in the freezer.

TO BAKE

4 Heat the oven to 350°F. Line two baking sheets with parchment paper. Using floured cookie cutters, cut out cookies and place them on the prepared sheets, spacing them 2 inches apart. Reroll, chill, and cut the scraps.

5 Bake, rotating the positions of the baking sheets halfway through, until cookies are light golden brown around edges, 10 to 12 minutes. Let cool on baking sheets for 5 minutes before transferring to a rack to cool completely.

Shortcut Sugar Cookie Cutouts

Skip straight to the rolling and shaping with this easy hack that turns slice-and-bake dough into holiday cutout cookies in no time.

Break one **16½-ounce package refrigerated ready-made sugar cookie dough** into pieces. On a well-floured surface, knead the dough until soft. Then knead **½ cup all-purpose flour** into the dough, a little at a time, until just incorporated. Form the dough into a disk. Lightly flour the rolling pin and your surface, then roll the dough to ¼ inch thick. Using floured cookie cutters, cut out cookies. Reroll, and repeat with the remaining dough. Transfer cutouts to a parchment paper-lined baking sheet, spacing them 2 inches apart. Freeze cookies on the prepared sheet for at least 30 minutes to help maintain their shape, then bake as the package directs.

Black Cocoa Cookie Dough

ACTIVE TIME 10 minutes

TOTAL TIME 10 minutes, plus chilling

MAKES 36 to 48 cookies (depending on size and shape)

- 2 cups all-purpose flour
- ¼ cup unsweetened cocoa powder, plus more for dusting
- ¼ cup unsweetened black cocoa powder
- ½ teaspoon baking soda
- ¼ teaspoon kosher salt
- ¾ cup (1½ sticks) unsalted butter, at room temperature
- ¾ cup sugar
- 1 large egg
- 2 teaspoons pure vanilla extract

OTHER MATERIALS

- Measuring cups and spoons
- Medium bowl
- Whisk
- Electric mixer
- Large bowl
- Parchment paper
- Rolling pin
- 2 baking sheets
- Cookie cutters
- Oven mitts
- Cooling rack

1. In a medium bowl, whisk together the flour, cocoa powders, baking soda, and salt; set aside.

2. Using an electric mixer, beat the butter and sugar in a large bowl on medium-high speed until fluffy, about 3 minutes. Beat in the egg and then the vanilla. Reduce the speed to low, and gradually add the flour mixture, mixing until fully incorporated.

3. Shape the dough into two 1-inch-thick disks, and roll each between two sheets of parchment paper to ⅛ to ¼ inch thick. Chill until firm, 30 minutes in the refrigerator or 15 minutes in the freezer.

TO BAKE

4. Heat the oven to 350°F. Line two baking sheets with parchment paper. Using cocoa-dusted cutters, cut out cookies. Place on the prepared sheets, spacing them 2 inches apart. Reroll, chill, and cut the scraps.

5. Bake, rotating the positions of the baking sheets halfway through, until cookies are light golden brown around edges, 10 to 12 minutes. Let cool on baking sheets for 5 minutes. Transfer to a cooling rack, and let cool completely.

Gingerbread Cookie Dough

ACTIVE TIME 10 minutes

TOTAL TIME 10 minutes, plus chilling

MAKES 36 to 48 cookies (depending on size and shape)

- 2½ cups all-purpose flour, plus more for dusting
- 2½ teaspoons ground ginger
- 1½ teaspoons cinnamon
- ½ teaspoon ground nutmeg
- ½ teaspoon baking soda
- ¼ teaspoon ground cloves
- ¼ teaspoon kosher salt
- ½ cup (1 stick) unsalted butter, at room temperature
- ½ cup firmly packed dark brown sugar
- 1 large egg
- ¼ cup molasses
- 1½ teaspoons pure vanilla extract

OTHER MATERIALS

- Measuring cups and spoons
- 2 large bowls
- Whisk
- Electric mixer
- Rolling pin
- Parchment paper
- 2 baking sheets
- Cookie cutters
- Oven mitts
- Cooling rack

1. In a large bowl, whisk together the flour, ginger, cinnamon, nutmeg, baking soda, cloves, and salt; set aside.

2. Using an electric mixer, beat the butter and sugar in a large bowl on medium-high speed until light and fluffy, about 3 minutes. Beat in the egg, molasses, and vanilla. Reduce speed to low, and gradually add the flour mixture, mixing until just incorporated (the dough will be soft).

3. Shape the dough into two 1-inch-thick disks. Roll each between two sheets of parchment paper, to ⅛ to ¼ inch thick. Chill until firm, 30 minutes in the refrigerator or 15 minutes in the freezer.

TO BAKE

4. Heat the oven to 350°F. Line two baking sheets with parchment paper. Using floured cookie cutters, cut out cookies and place them on the prepared sheets, spacing them 1 inch apart. Reroll, chill, and cut the scraps. Chill cookies for 10 minutes before baking.

5. Bake, rotating the pans halfway through, until the cookies are set and the edges are beginning to brown, 12 to 15 minutes. Let cool on the baking sheets for 3 minutes. Transfer to a cooling rack, and let cool completely.

Chocolate Buttons

ACTIVE TIME 35 minutes
TOTAL TIME 3 hours
MAKES 48

- 2½ cups all-purpose flour
- 1 teaspoon baking powder
- ¼ teaspoon kosher salt
- ¾ cup (1½ sticks) unsalted butter, at room temperature
- 1¼ cups sugar
- 1 large egg, plus 1 egg yolk
- 3 teaspoons pure vanilla extract, divided
- 5 ounces unsweetened chocolate, divided
- 3 cups confectioners' sugar
- 2 tablespoons unsweetened cocoa powder
- 2 teaspoons light corn syrup

OTHER MATERIALS

- Medium bowl
- Measuring cups and spoons
- Whisk
- Electric mixer
- 1 large bowl
- 2 small microwave-safe bowls
- 2 baking sheets
- Parchment paper
- Drinking glass
- Reusable straw
- Oven mitts
- Cooling rack
- Wooden skewer
- Wire rack
- Waxed paper
- Thin satin ribbon (for garland)

1 In a medium bowl, whisk together the flour, baking powder, and salt. Set aside.

2 Using an electric mixer, beat the butter and sugar in a large bowl on medium speed until light and fluffy, about 3 minutes. Beat in the egg, yolk, and 2 teaspoons vanilla.

3 In a small, microwave-safe bowl, melt 3 ounces chocolate in the microwave according to package directions. Reduce mixer speed to low, and mix in the melted chocolate. Gradually add the flour mixture, mixing until just incorporated. Cover, and refrigerate until dough is firm enough to handle, about 1 hour.

4 Heat the oven to 350°F. Line 2 baking sheets with parchment paper.

5 Roll level tablespoons of dough into balls. Place on baking sheets, spacing them 1½ inches apart. Using the bottom of a glass, flatten the balls into 1½-inch disks. Use a reusable straw to poke four holes through the center of each cookie so it resembles a button.

6 Bake, rotating the positions of the baking sheets halfway through, until the cookies' edges are set but centers are still slightly soft, 10 to 12 minutes. Let cool on baking sheets for 5 minutes. Transfer to a cooling rack, and let cool completely. (While the cookies are warm, use a wooden skewer to reopen any holes.)

7 In a small, microwave-safe bowl, melt the remaining 2 ounces chocolate in the microwave in 30-second intervals until smooth. In a large bowl, sift the confectioners' sugar and cocoa. Add the melted chocolate, corn syrup, 6 tablespoons hot water, and the remaining teaspoon vanilla; stir until smooth.

8 Place a wire rack over a piece of waxed paper. Dip the face of each cookie in the chocolate glaze, let the excess drip off, then place it on the rack. (Use a skewer to reopen any holes.) Let set for 1 hour.

From Baking to Decorating!
You can use these cute-as-a-button cookies to make an edible garland. Thread satin ribbon through the button holes, and hang your garland along a doorway or on your tree. (We won't tell if you take a nibble!)

Tree-Light Cookies

ACTIVE TIME 1 hour 40 minutes
TOTAL TIME 2 hours 40 minutes
MAKES 36 to 48 (depending on size and shape)

- 1 batch Classic Sugar Cookie Dough (page 113)
- Flour, for coating and work surface
- Decorating Icing (see box at right)

OTHER MATERIALS

- 3-inch tree-light-shaped cookie cutter
- Reusable straw
- Toothpick
- Ribbon

1 Prepare cookie dough according to recipe instructions, using a flour-coated tree-light-shaped cookie cutter to cut out shapes. Use a reusable straw to make a small hole at the base of each cookie light. Bake, and let cool completely before decorating.

2 Time to decorate! With slow, steady pressure, squeeze decorating icing from the piping bag to outline the cookie (or the area) you want to ice. Let the outline dry.

3 "Flood" your cookies: Squeeze some icing into the center of the outlined area, and use a toothpick to drag it to the outlined edge. Repeat with the other colors you'd like in your string of cookie lights. Once the icing is dry, finish by tying a ribbon through the hole at the base of each cookie.

Decorating Icing

Using an electric mixer, beat **16 ounces confectioners' sugar, 3 tablespoons meringue powder** and **⅓ cup warm water** in a large bowl on medium speed until blended and mixture is very stiff, about 5 minutes. Tint icing with **gel food coloring** if desired, then press plastic wrap directly onto surface to prevent it from drying out. When ready to decorate, fill piping bags fitted with small tips to ice cookies. Makes 3 cups.

Mini Chocolate Chip Sandwiches

ACTIVE TIME 25 minutes
TOTAL TIME 35 minutes
MAKES 25

- 1½ cups cake flour
- ½ teaspoon baking powder
- ½ teaspoon baking soda
- ½ teaspoon kosher salt
- ½ cup (1 stick) unsalted butter, at room temperature
- ¼ cup plus 2 tablespoons granulated sugar
- 2 tablespoons packed light brown sugar
- 1 large egg
- ½ teaspoon pure vanilla extract
- 4 ounces bittersweet chocolate, roughly chopped
- 4 ounces semisweet chocolate, roughly chopped
- Prepared chocolate frosting, for assembly

OTHER MATERIALS

- 2 large baking sheets
- Parchment paper
- Measuring cups and spoons
- Medium bowl
- Sifter
- Electric mixer
- Large bowl
- Rubber spatula
- Oven mitts
- Butter knife

1   Line two large baking sheets with parchment paper. In a medium bowl, sift together cake flour, baking powder, baking soda, and salt; set aside.

2   Using an electric mixer, beat butter and sugars in a large bowl on medium speed until light and fluffy, 3 minutes. Reduce speed to low, and beat in the egg and then the vanilla.

3   Add the flour mixture in three batches, mixing until just incorporated. Fold in chocolates.

4   Scoop rounded teaspoons of dough onto the prepared baking sheets, arranging the cookies 2 inches apart. Flatten the tops slightly with your hands, and freeze for 10 minutes.

5   Heat the oven to 350°F. Bake, rotating pans after 5 minutes, until cookies are puffed and edges are beginning to turn golden brown, 7 to 8 minutes total. Let cool completely.

6   Time to assemble! Use a butter knife to spread chocolate frosting on the bottom of half the cookies, then top with the remaining cookies.

Cranberry Shortbread Cookies

ACTIVE TIME 20 minutes
TOTAL TIME 1 hour 20 minutes
MAKES 28

- ⅓ cup sugar
- ¼ teaspoon chopped fresh rosemary
- ⅓ cup frozen cranberries (about 1½ ounces)
- ¾ cup (1½ sticks) unsalted butter, at room temperature
- ½ teaspoon pure vanilla extract
- 1 teaspoon finely grated orange zest
- 1½ cups all-purpose flour
- ¼ teaspoon kosher salt

OTHER MATERIALS

- 2 baking sheets
- Parchment paper
- Measuring cups and spoons
- Food processor
- Large bowl
- Paper towel
- Electric mixer
- Plastic wrap
- Rolling pin
- Oven mitts

1. Line two baking sheets with parchment paper. In a food processor, pulse sugar and rosemary until very finely chopped. Transfer the rosemary sugar to a large bowl. Wipe out the food processor with a paper towel. Add the frozen cranberries, and pulse to break them into pea-size pieces.

2. Using an electric mixer, beat the butter and rosemary sugar on medium speed until very well combined. Beat in the vanilla and zest.

3. Reduce the speed to low, and gradually add the flour and salt, mixing until just incorporated. Fold in chopped cranberries. The dough should look streaky with bits of cranberries.

4. On a piece of plastic wrap, form dough into a 7½-by-2¾-by-1-inch-thick rectangle. Freeze or refrigerate until firm, about 45 minutes in the freezer or 2 hours in the fridge.

5. Heat the oven to 325°F. Slice dough into ¼-inch-thick rectangles, and transfer to the baking sheet, spacing them 2 inches apart. Bake, rotating the positions of the baking sheets halfway through, until light-golden brown, 15 to 18 minutes. Let cool completely on the baking sheets.

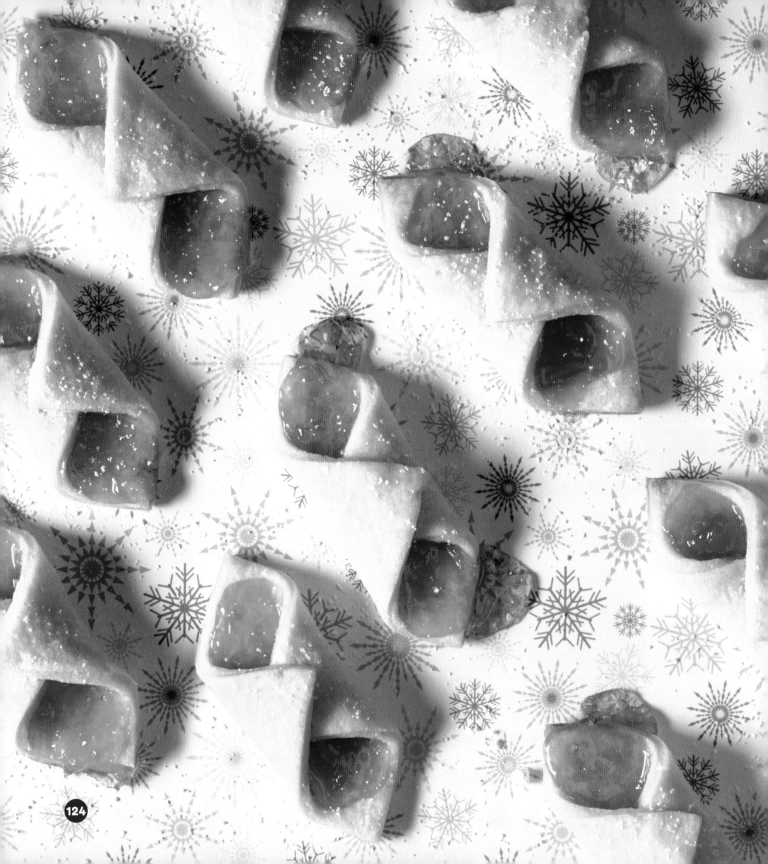

Apricot Kolaches

ACTIVE TIME 1 hour
TOTAL TIME 1 hour 10 minutes, plus chilling
MAKES 60 cookies

- 1¼ cups all-purpose flour, plus more for work surface
- ¼ cup sugar
- ¼ teaspoon kosher salt
- ½ cup (1 stick) cold unsalted butter, cut up
- ¼ cup sour cream
- 1 large egg yolk
- ⅔ cup apricot jam

OTHER MATERIALS

- Measuring cups and spoons
- Large bowl
- Whisk
- Butter knife
- Mixing spoon
- Rolling pin
- Plastic wrap
- 2 baking sheets
- Parchment paper
- Sharp knife
- Spoon
- Oven mitts
- Wire rack

1 In a large bowl, whisk together flour, sugar, and salt.

2 With a butter knife, cut in butter until the mixture resembles coarse crumbs. Stir in sour cream and egg yolk, mixing until fully combined.

3 Turn the dough out onto a floured work surface, and knead until smooth, 3 to 4 minutes. Using a rolling pin, shape the dough into two ¾-inch-thick disks. Wrap the disks in plastic, and chill until firm, at least 2 hours and up to overnight in the refrigerator.

4 Heat oven to 375°F. Line two baking sheets with parchment paper. Working on a lightly floured surface with one disk of dough at a time, roll to ⅛ inch thick. With a sharp knife, cut the dough into 2-inch squares.

5 Place ½ teaspoon apricot jam diagonally across each dough square. Dab pointer fingers in water, and moisten the two opposite corners of the dough without jam. Press the corners together to seal. Place cookies on prepared baking sheets. Repeat with the remaining disk. Reroll, chill, and cut scraps.

6 Bake, rotating the positions of the baking sheets halfway through, until edges are light golden brown, 10 to 12 minutes. Transfer cookies to a wire rack, and let cool completely.

Kolaches (pronounced "ko-lah-chee") can be found in bakeries across eastern Europe. Czech Republic immigrants brought these jam-filled treats to the southern United States, where they became Christmas cookie staples.

Cream Cheese Spritz Cookies

ACTIVE TIME 30 minutes
TOTAL TIME 1 hour
MAKES 90

- 1 cup (2 sticks) unsalted butter, at room temperature
- 1 cup sugar
- 3 ounces cream cheese, at room temperature
- 1 large egg yolk
- 1 teaspoon pure vanilla extract
- Green and red food coloring (optional)
- 2½ cups all-purpose flour
- ¼ teaspoon kosher salt

OTHER MATERIALS

- Measuring cups and spoons
- Electric mixer
- Large bowl
- Cookie press(es)
- 2 baking sheets
- Oven mitts
- Wire racks
- Icing and sprinkles, for decorating

1   Heat the oven to 350°F. Using an electric mixer, beat the butter, sugar, and cream cheese in a large bowl on medium speed until light and fluffy, about 3 minutes. Beat in the egg yolk and vanilla, then the food coloring if you'd like. Stir in the flour and salt until just incorporated.

2   Fill a cookie press according to manufacturer's instructions. Using two unlined baking sheets and holding the cookie press so it touches the sheet, squeeze and lift away, spacing cookies 1 inch apart. Bake, rotating baking sheets halfway through, until edges are light-golden brown, 15 to 17 minutes.

3   Let the cookies cool on sheets for 1 minute. Transfer to wire racks, and let cool completely. Repeat with remaining dough (rinsing sheets with cold water to help them cool). Decorate as desired.

No Cookie Press? No Problem!

Fill a large piping bag, and fit it with a large open-star tip. Pipe the dough into 2-inch logs onto baking sheets, spacing them 2 inches apart.

Jam Sandwiches

ACTIVE TIME 35 minutes
TOTAL TIME 50 minutes, plus chilling
MAKES 18 to 24

- 1 batch Classic Sugar Cookie Dough (page 113)

- All-purpose flour, for work surface

- Apricot, orange, or raspberry jam, for spreading

- Confectioners' sugar, for dusting

OTHER MATERIALS

- Rolling pin

- 2-inch cookie cutter

- 1-inch cookie cutter

- Spoon

- Oven mitts

- Sifter

1 Prepare cookie dough, following recipe instructions through step 3, but divide the dough into two disks.

2 Sprinkle a clean work surface with flour, then roll out one disk of dough to about ⅛ inch thick. Using a floured 2-inch cookie cutter, cut out cookies. Using a floured smaller cutter, cut out the centers of half the cookies. Bake as directed.

3 Spread each whole cookie with 1½ teaspoons jam, and top each with one cutout. Dust the cooled cutout cookies with confectioners' sugar.

Crispy Corn Flake Wreaths

ACTIVE TIME 20 minutes

TOTAL TIME 20 minutes

MAKES 36 cookies

- ½ cup (1 stick) unsalted butter

- 12 ounces marshmallows

- ½ teaspoon green gel food coloring

- ½ teaspoon pure peppermint extract

- 4 cups Corn Flakes cereal

- Sprinkles or mini candy-coated chocolates (such as M&M's)

OTHER MATERIALS

- Large saucepan

- Measuring cups and spoons

- Mixing spoon

- Nonstick pan

- Foil

1   In a large saucepan, melt butter on low. Add marshmallows and food coloring, and cook, stirring, until melted and combined. Remove from heat; stir in peppermint and cornflakes.

2   Using wet hands, form 3- to 4-inch disks on a nonstick foil-lined pan, then poke a hole in the middle of each with your finger. Working quickly, repeat with the remaining mixture. Scatter with sprinkles or candies, then leave in a cool place to set, 2 to 3 hours. Store in an air-tight container for up to 3 days.

White Chocolate Peppermint Patties

ACTIVE TIME 25 minutes
TOTAL TIME 1 hour 10 minutes
MAKES 30

- 4 cups confectioners' sugar
- 4 tablespoons unsalted butter, at room temperature
- ¼ cup heavy cream
- 1½ teaspoons pure peppermint extract
- ½ teaspoon pure vanilla extract
- ½ teaspoon kosher salt
- 12 ounces white chocolate, chopped
- 2 tablespoons solid coconut oil
- Crushed peppermint candies, for sprinkling

OTHER MATERIALS
- 2 baking sheets
- Parchment paper
- Electric mixer
- Measuring cups and spoons
- Large bowl
- Drinking glass
- Grease
- Waxed paper
- Medium bowl
- Fork

1. Line two baking sheets with parchment paper. Using an electric mixer, beat the confectioners' sugar, butter, cream, peppermint, vanilla, and salt in a large bowl on low speed until smooth, 1 to 2 minutes.

2. Roll the mixture into 30 balls. Place on prepared baking sheets, and flatten into ¼-inch-thick disks using a drinking glass and a greased piece of waxed paper. Cover, and freeze 30 minutes.

3. In a medium bowl, microwave white chocolate and coconut oil in 30-second increments, stirring in between, until melted.

4. Place one chilled peppermint disk on the end of a fork, and dip it into melted chocolate, gently tapping off excess. Return the disk to the baking sheet, and repeat with the remaining peppermint disks. Sprinkle tops with crushed peppermint. Chill until set, 15 to 20 minutes. Store refrigerated in an airtight container for up to 1 week.

Sugar Cookie Trees

ACTIVE TIME 30 minutes, plus decorating

TOTAL TIME: 45 minutes

MAKES About 6

- 1 batch Classic Sugar Cookie Dough (page 113)
- All-purpose flour, for work surface
- Green gel food coloring
- Decorating Icing (page 119)
- Chocolate caramel candies
- Confectioners' sugar, for dusting (optional)

OTHER MATERIALS

- Plastic wrap
- Parchment paper
- Rolling pin
- Mixing spoon
- Round cookie cutters in different sizes
- 2 baking sheets
- Oven mitts
- Wire racks
- Mini star cookie cutter

1. Prepare cookie dough according to recipe instructions. Sprinkle a clean work surface with flour. Divide dough into four equal portions. Wrap all but one dough portion in plastic.

2. Working with one portion at a time, add a couple of drops of green food coloring to the dough, and mix until fully incorporated. (A helpful hint: Tint the dough slightly darker than you want your final cookies to be; the cookies will bake up lighter.) Roll the dough between two sheets of parchment paper, to ⅛ inch thick. Chill until firm, 30 minutes in the refrigerator or 15 minutes in the freezer. Repeat with two more sections of dough, using different amounts of food coloring to create the light and dark shades shown in the photo. Divide the fourth portion of dough in half. Color half green, and repeat above. Save the last, undyed portion for step 5.

3. Heat the oven to 350°F. Line two baking sheets with parchment paper. Using floured cookie cutters, cut out cookies for the tree. To ensure your tree is sturdy, plan for two cookies on each layer of the tree. Continue with smaller cookie cutters until you have four layers for a tree (eight cookies in total).

4. Bake, rotating positions of baking sheets halfway through, until cookies are light-golden brown around the edges, 10 to 12 minutes. Let cool on sheets for 5 minutes. Transfer to wire racks, and let cool completely.

5. While the tree layers are baking, reroll the final portion of dough, and cut one mini star for each tree. Bake until cookie stars are light-golden brown, about 6 minutes.

6. Use Decorating Icing to "glue" cookies together in tree shapes: alternate light and dark shades of green in four layers, with two cookies per layer; glue stars at the tops and chocolate caramels as trunks. Dust with confectioners' sugar if desired.

133

Red Velvet Cookies

ACTIVE TIME 15 minutes
TOTAL TIME 45 minutes
MAKES 30

- 2 cups all-purpose flour
- ½ cup Dutch-process cocoa powder
- 1 teaspoon baking soda
- 1 teaspoon kosher salt
- 1 cup (2 sticks) unsalted butter, at room temperature
- ¾ cup packed light brown sugar
- ½ cup granulated sugar
- 1 large egg
- 1 teaspoon red gel food coloring
- 2 teaspoons pure vanilla extract
- 12 ounces semisweet chocolate chips

OTHER MATERIALS

- 2 baking sheets
- Parchment paper
- 2 large bowls
- Measuring cups and spoons
- Whisk
- Electric mixer
- Mixing spoon
- Oven mitts
- Wire rack

1 Heat the oven to 350°F. Line two baking sheets with parchment paper. In a large bowl, whisk together the flour, cocoa, baking soda, and salt.

2 Using an electric mixer on medium speed, in a large bowl beat together the butter and sugars until combined. Add the egg, food coloring, and vanilla, and mix until just combined.

3 Reduce the mixer speed to low, and add the flour mixture until just combined. Fold in chocolate chips.

4 Scoop heaping spoonfuls of dough onto the prepared baking sheets, spacing the dough 1½ inches apart.

5 Bake the cookies, rotating the positions of the pans on racks halfway through, until darker around the edges, 9 to 12 minutes total.

6 Let cool 5 minutes on pans. Slide the parchment paper and cookies onto a wire rack, and let cool at least 5 minutes more before serving.

Share the Sweetness!

National Cookie Exchange Day is December 22. Celebrate the occasion by hosting a cookie swap for you and your friends.

1 Ask each guest you invite to the party to bring two dozen of their favorite homemade holiday cookie.

2 Set up a table at your house where each party guest can place their cookies.

3 Have treat bags or boxes so friends can take a few of each cookie when they leave.

Add to the festivities by playing one of these games at the party!

Don't Say "Cookie" As guests arrive, give them a small item they can wear, such as a jingle bell necklace or a candy bracelet. Then challenge everyone to avoid saying the word *cookie* during the party. If someone does, they lose their trinket to the person who heard them. The guest with the most flair at the end of the party wins.

Smart Cookie Memory Game
Have your guests sit in a circle. Draw a number to see who will go first. This person will start by saying the name of the cookie they brought to the party. The guest to their right then has to repeat the first person's cookie, plus say their own. Go around the circle until you reach the first person, who must name all the other cookies.

GINGERBREAD HEADQUARTERS

Run, run, as fast as you can: It's time to bake* a batch of gingerbread and decorate your very own house!

*Starting with a store-bought kit is also holiday approved!

The Story of the Gingerbread House

The Brothers Grimm tale of Hansel and Gretel may be behind our tradition of decorating gingerbread houses. The story of the brother and sister who stumble upon a witch's home built from gingerbread originated in 16th-century Germany, which was around the time people began making gingerbread houses to display and enjoy during the holidays. It's unknown which came first—the story or the practice—but historians say the two are connected. Before then, cookies baked with ginger and molasses or honey were already a common winter treat, thanks to the spicy, warming qualities of ginger.

Make-It-From-Scratch Gingerbread House

If you want to construct your house from the oven up...

- **2 batches dough for Gingerbread Cookie Dough (page 115)**

OTHER MATERIALS

- Rolling pin
- Plastic wrap
- 3 rimmed baking sheets
- Parchment paper
- Gingerbread house templates (scan the smart code)
- Scissors
- All-purpose flour, for work surface
- Pizza wheel or sharp knife
- Oven mitts
- Wire racks

SCAN HERE

1   Divide gingerbread dough into four pieces, and form each into 1-inch-thick disk; wrap each disk in plastic. Refrigerate until firm, at least 4 hours and up to 2 days.

2   Heat the oven to 375°F with a rack in the center. Line three rimmed baking sheets with parchment paper.

3   Use scissors to cut out the printed gingerbread house templates. Working with 1 disk at a time, roll the dough on a lightly floured work surface to ⅛ to ¼ inch thick. Use a pizza wheel or sharp knife to trace templates into the dough, cutting two of each shape. (Gather and refrigerate scraps while working with remaining dough; they can be rerolled once.) Transfer gingerbread cutouts to prepared baking sheets, leaving 1 inch of space around each, and freeze until firm, 15 minutes.

4   Bake gingerbread one tray at a time, until puffed and firm, 25 to 30 minutes. Let cool on baking sheets 5 minutes. Transfer to wire racks, and let cool completely.

When You're Ready to Decorate

Whether you've baked your own gingerbread house or are starting with a ready-made kit, these crafty details are sure to make it a home sweet home. (Emphasis on the sweet!)

Evergreen Wreath Slice gumdrops, fan them out into a circle (with slices overlapping), and "glue" them together with icing.

Red Roof To make these bright shingles, slightly overlap layers of red Sour Power belt pieces using cookie icing or decorating icing (page 119) as glue.

Shingled Roof Make a more rustic roof style by overlapping sliced almonds, which resembles the look of cedar.

Fresh Greenery Sprigs of herbs like rosemary or thyme make an easy garland.

Stained-Glass Windows Bake crushed hard candies in greased cookie cutters at 350°F until melted. Then let cool completely, and pop out of the molds. Attach to walls of gingerbread house with decorating icing (page 119).

Mounted Antlers Divide a knotted pretzel in two, and mount the pieces to the front of the house with a dab of royal icing.

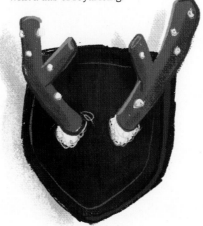

Stone Chimney Make a chimney base using four pieces of graham crackers. (You may need to cut the bottoms at an angle, depending on the slope of your roof.) Attach the four pieces together using decorating icing (page 119), and let dry. Then coat the chimney with additional icing, and add speckled white jellybeans. Let set before attaching to the house with remaining decorating icing.

Log Walls Use royal icing to attach long Tootsie Rolls to the sides of your house, cutting to fit as needed.

Rocky Road "Pave" a path with chocolate rocks and candy pebbles.

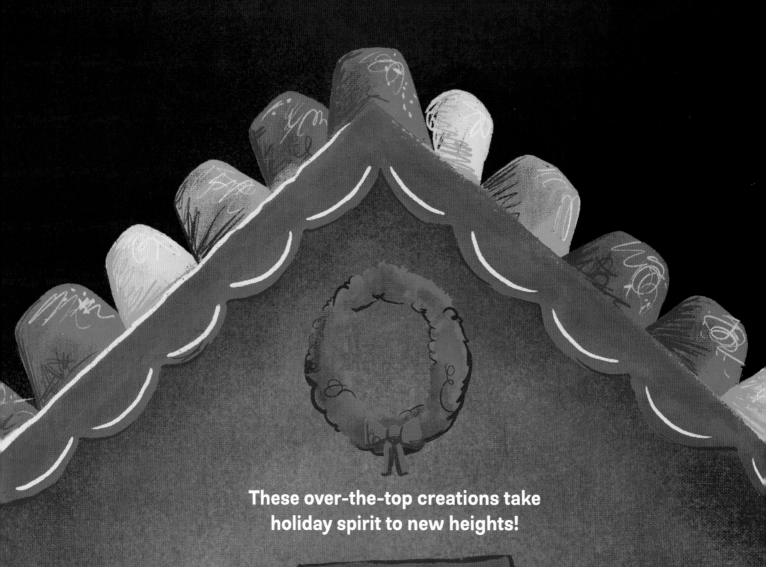

Gingerbread House
Hall of Fame

These over-the-top creations take
holiday spirit to new heights!

Presidential Seal of Approval

Displayed in the State Dining Room, the White House gingerbread house has been an annual Christmas tradition for more than 50 years ago. A recent creation featured a snow-covered, wreath-adorned replica of the executive mansion.

Checking In

Throughout the United States, hotels craft life-size gingerbread houses that you can step inside, from the Rancho Bernardo Inn in San Diego to the **Grand Floridian** at Walt Disney World. Warning: Visits to these may flare up your sweet tooth.

Down the Lane

Each year Jon Lovitch, a chef in New York, creates more than 1,500 gingerbread structures for his massive and merry gingerbread village. He starts working in January to be ready for the following Christmas. Displayed at the Essex Market in Manhattan, the installation features, on average, 610 pounds of gingerbread, 3,740 pounds of frosting, and 810 pounds of candy.

Best in Show

The National Gingerbread House Competition takes place each year in Asheville, North Carolina. Bakers of all ages gather from around the country to compete for top honors. Some winners feature quirky characters (Baby Yoda once made an appearance!) and complicated mechanics (a rotating carousel!), while this merry holiday scene was prized for its classic Christmas cheer. Maybe next year the winner will be you!

Snow
MUCH
FUN

Get ready for a flurry of tasty fun with these snowman-themed sweets and snacks.

Eggnog Mousse Snowmen

ACTIVE TIME 20 minutes
TOTAL TIME 1 hour, 50 minutes
(plus cooling)
MAKES 8

FOR THE MOUSSE

- 2½ cups cold heavy cream, divided
- 1½ cinnamon sticks
- 6 cloves
- 5 gratings whole nutmeg
- 20 marshmallows
- 3 tablespoons unsalted butter
- 4 ounces white chocolate, chopped

FOR THE CHOCOLATE DECORATION

- 2 ounces semisweet chocolate chips
- 1 ounce red candy melts

FOR THE FROSTING AND FACES

- 4 large egg whites
- 1 cup sugar
- ¼ teaspoon cream of tartar
- Pinch of salt
- 33 mini chocolate chips
- 8 orange jelly beans

1. Make the mousse: In a small saucepan, heat ½ cup heavy cream, cinnamon, cloves, and nutmeg until bubbling around the edges, about 4 minutes. Remove from the heat, and let spices steep at least 1 hour.

2. Strain spiced cream into a large bowl. Add the marshmallows, butter, and white chocolate, and microwave on high in 30-second intervals, stirring occasionally, until completely melted and smooth. Let cool to room temperature, about 30 minutes.

3. Using an electric mixer, beat the remaining 2 cups heavy cream until stiff peaks form. Fold whipped cream into the marshmallow mixture. Set aside.

4. Make the chocolate decorations: In a small bowl, microwave chocolate chips on high in 30-second intervals, stirring occasionally, until melted and smooth. Let cool slightly to thicken, then transfer to a resealable bag and cut off one corner to make a small hole. Pipe arms and

OTHER MATERIALS

- Small saucepan
- Measuring cups and spoons
- Oven mitts
- Mixing spoon
- Strainer
- Large bowl
- Electric mixer
- Small bowl
- Resealable plastic bag, for piping
- Pot
- Small glass canning jars
- Electric stand mixer
- Whisk
- Large piping bag
- Large round piping tip

buttons into the insides of the jars. (Use the photo as your guide.)

5. Repeat step 4 with the candy melts. Pipe bow ties and scarves (or other accessories) on the outside of the jars. Let chocolate decorations set, about 5 minutes.

6. Once set, transfer the mousse to glasses, and refrigerate.

7. Prepare the frosting: Fill a pot with 1 to 2 inches water, and bring to barely a simmer. Place the bowl of an electric stand mixer over the simmering water. Add egg whites, sugar, cream of tartar, and salt, and whisk until sugar dissolves. Transfer the bowl to the stand mixer, and whisk on medium-high speed until stiff, glossy peaks form. Spoon frosting into a large piping bag fitted with a large round tip. Pipe snowman heads. Add mini chocolate chips for eyes and jellybeans for noses.

WHY DO SNOWMEN LIKE LIVING AT THE NORTH POLE?

BECAUSE IT'S COOL!

Snow People Cupcakes

ACTIVE TIME 45 minutes

TOTAL TIME 1 hour, plus chilling and decorating

MAKES 6 to 7

FOR THE CUPCAKES

- One box store-bought vanilla cake mix
- One can store-bought vanilla frosting

FOR THE DECORATIONS

- 3 cups shredded coconut
- Dark chocolate frosting
- Thin sandwich cookies (such as Oreo Thins)
- Mini sandwich cookies (such as Mini Oreos)
- Flower sprinkles
- Sour belts in various colors
- ¼ cup yellow candy melts
- Pretzel sticks
- ¼ cup potato sticks
- Mini candy-coated chocolates (such as mini M&M's)
- Candy-coated chocolates (such as M&M's)
- Gumdrops

OTHER MATERIALS

- Mini, standard, and jumbo cupcake pans
- Paper cupcake liners
- Toothpick
- Oven mitts
- Wire rack
- Measuring cups and spoons
- Shallow bowl
- 2 piping bags
- 2 round plain #2 decorating tips
- Kitchen scissors
- Microwave-safe bowl
- Waxed paper

FOR THE CUPCAKES

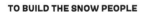

1. Prepare cupcake batter according to store-bought cake mix package instructions.

2. Divide batter among six mini, six standard, and six jumbo cupcake pan cups, each lined with paper liners. Bake until a toothpick inserted in the center of each cupcake comes out clean, 18 to 22 minutes, with less time for the mini cupcakes and more for jumbo ones. Transfer to a wire rack, and let cool completely. Chill before decorating.

TO BUILD THE SNOW PEOPLE

3. Place coconut in a shallow bowl. Spread a generous mound of frosting on top of one chilled jumbo cupcake, and smooth. Gently roll the top in coconut to coat. Reshape frosting to make it smooth if necessary.

4. Repeat with one standard and one mini cupcake. Add a dot of frosting on top of the jumbo and standard cupcakes. Stack the flat side of the standard cupcake into the frosting of the jumbo one, pressing to secure, and place the mini cupcake on its side on top.

5. Place the cupcake stack in the fridge to set. Repeat with the remaining cupcakes, arranging stacks as you wish. Makes 6 three-tiered cupcakes.

TIME TO DECORATE!

6. Remove snow family from the refrigerator. Use the candies and treats you've gathered to "dress" them up:

   - *To make eyes, noses, buttons, and earmuffs:* Press mini and regular M&M's into the vanilla frosting.

   - *To make hats, scarves, and ties:* Cut sour belts into desired shapes.

   - *To make the black hat:* Spoon dark chocolate frosting into a piping bag fitted with a pastry tip. Pipe a dot of chocolate frosting on top of a thin cookie, and stick a mini cookie on top. Add a flower sprinkle.

   - *To make the red ball cap:* Cut a piece of red sour belt into a 2-inch oval, and attach it to the flat side of a red gumdrop. Spoon dark chocolate frosting into a piping bag fitted with a piping tip, and pipe an initial onto the cap. (Like F for Frosty!)

   - *To make the broom:* Place candy melts in a microwave-safe bowl, and heat, stirring every 10 seconds, until smooth. Spoon a small dot onto a sheet of waxed paper. Place 1 end of a pretzel stick into the candy, and arrange potato sticks vertically as bristles at the bottom. Attach a thin strip of red sour belt crosswise on bristles; let dry.

7. After the "clothing" decorations are complete, finish by piping chocolate smiles onto faces.

Snowy Cookie Truffles

ACTIVE TIME 30 minutes, plus decorating
TOTAL TIME 30 minutes, plus decorating
MAKES 18

FOR THE TRUFFLES

- 14.3-ounce package sandwich cookies (such as Oreos)
- 8 ounces cream cheese, room temperature
- 14 ounces white chocolate chips
- ½ teaspoon vegetable oil

FOR THE DECORATIONS

- Red, green, and white candy melts
- Chocolate and vanilla frosting
- Shredded coconut
- Nonpareil sprinkles
- Fruit leather
- Spice drops
- White Smarties
- Mini candy-coated chocolates (such as mini M&M's)
- Semisweet chocolate, melted
- Mini sandwich cookies (such as Oreo Minis)
- Black sanding sugar
- Red candy-coated chocolates (such as M&M's)
- Pretzels

OTHER MATERIALS

- Large baking sheet
- Parchment paper
- Food processor
- Small, microwave-safe measuring cup
- Measuring spoons
- Oven mitts
- Wooden picks
- Piping bags and tips
- Butter knife

FOR THE TRUFFLES

1 Line a baking sheet with parchment paper. In a food processor, pulse cookies to form fine crumbs. Add cream cheese, and pulse until the mixture forms a ball. Form mixture into 18 balls (about 1¼ ounces each), and transfer to the prepared baking sheet. Freeze until firm, 15 to 20 minutes. Reroll balls to make smooth surfaces, and return to freezer.

2 Place white chocolate in a small measuring cup, and microwave at 50% power in 30-second increments, stirring in between, until melted and smooth. Stir in vegetable oil. Working one at a time, stick a wooden pick into each truffle ball, and spoon chocolate over it; gently tap off excess. Transfer to the prepared baking sheet, remove the stick, and refrigerate until all balls are completed.

FOR THE SNOWMEN DECORATION

1 For hats, dip the top third of the white chocolate–coated ball in red or green melted candy melts, and let the excess drip to the tip to create the top of the "hat"; let set.

2 Pipe a line of frosting around the hat, and sprinkle with nonpareils or shredded coconut.

3 To add earmuffs, cut a strip of fruit leather for the band across the top. Add a slice of spice drop or gumdrop for the ear coverings. Attach with melted white chocolate. Then pipe chocolate-frosting eyes and a mouth. Add an orange spice drop wedge for the nose.

FOR THE POLAR BEAR DECORATION

1 Immediately after dipping truffles into chocolate, sprinkle with shredded coconut to coat completely; let set.

2 Using additional melted chocolate or frosting as "glue," stick on white Smarties for ears and a white candy melt as the muzzle, sticking a mini brown candy-coated chocolate onto the candy melt for the nose. Then pipe chocolate frosting on for the eyes.

FOR THE PENGUIN DECORATION

1 Dip one side of the white chocolate–coated ball into melted semisweet chocolate; let set.

2 Use a butter knife to scrape the cream off one mini sandwich cookie, and cut cookie in half. Brush some melted chocolate on flat side of the halves, and dip them into black sanding sugar to make wings.

3 Cut a thin slice from the flat side of an orange spice drop, and cut the slice in half to make feet (two semicircles). Cut a small wedge from the remaining part for the beak.

4 Attach the wings with some melted chocolate on the sides of the penguin. Pipe chocolate-frosting eyes. Attach feet and beak with some white chocolate.

FOR THE REINDEER DECORATION

1 Use melted chocolate to glue on a candy-coated chocolate for the nose.

2 Then use a wooden pick to make a hole on each side of the ball, and press in pretzel halves for antlers.

3 Use vanilla frosting to add tufts of hair, and attach holly sprinkles between the antlers. Pipe on chocolate frosting for eyes, and stick on a candy-coated chocolate for the nose.

Snowman Spoons

ACTIVE TIME 15 minutes
TOTAL TIME 15 minutes
MAKES 8

- 4 ounces semisweet chocolate, chopped
- Candy cane spoons (available online or in specialty stores)
- Mini marshmallows
- Mini and regular chocolate chips
- Snowcaps
- Pretzel sticks
- Hot chocolate, for serving

OTHER MATERIALS

- Large baking sheet
- Parchment paper
- Small microwave-safe bowl
- Oven mitts

1   Line a large baking sheet with parchment paper. In a small bowl, microwave chocolate on high in 30-second intervals, stirring occasionally, until melted and smooth.

2   Working one at a time, dip each spoon into melted chocolate, tap off excess, and transfer to prepared baking sheet.

3   Time to decorate! Create bodies with three mini marshmallows. Press in mini chocolate chip eyes, chocolate chip or snowcap hats, and small pretzel pieces as arms. Serve with hot chocolate.

148

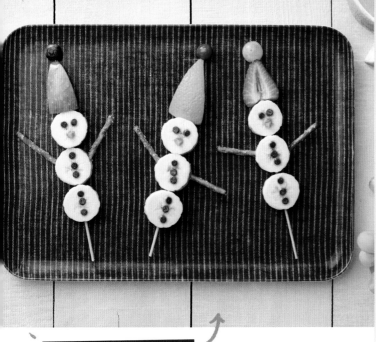

Melting Snowmen

ACTIVE TIME 25 minutes
TOTAL TIME 25 minutes
MAKES 8

- 12 ounces premium white chocolate chips
- 4 mini sandwich cookies (such as Oreo Minis)
- 16 ounces store-bought vanilla frosting
- Black licorice
- Orange chewy candies (such as Starburst)
- Mini chocolate chips
- Pretzel sticks
- Candy-coated chocolates (such as M&M's)
- Shoestring licorice

OTHER MATERIALS

- Lage baking sheet
- Parchment paper
- Medium microwave-safe bowl
- Tablespoon
- Oven mitts
- Wooden ice pop sticks

1 Line a large baking sheet with parchment paper.

2 In a medium bowl, microwave white chocolate chips on high in 30-second intervals, stirring occasionally, until melted and smooth.

3 Spoon 2 tablespoons chocolate into eight separate pools on a prepared baking sheet. Make slightly larger mounds where heads should be.

4 Press ice-pop stick two-thirds into each chocolate pool, and cover with more chocolate.

5 To make top hats, separate four Oreo Minis, and scrape off and discard the filling. Using the icing as "glue," adhere a small slice of round black licorice to the center of each cookie.

6 Decorate the snowmen using orange chewy candies for the nose, chocolate chips for the eyes, pretzels for the arms, candy-coated chocolates for buttons, and licorice for scarves. Let set, and enjoy.

Banana Snowmen

ACTIVE TIME 10 minutes
TOTAL TIME 10 minutes
MAKES 3 (or more!)

- Blueberry, cranberry, or grape, washed and sliced
- Apple, orange, or strawberry, washed and sliced
- Banana, sliced thick
- Mini chocolate chips
- Baby carrot, washed and cut into nose-shaped slivers
- Pretzel sticks

OTHER MATERIALS

- Wooden skewer

1 Slide the "hat pom-pom" (blueberry, cranberry, or grape) to one end of the skewer.

2 Slide the "hat" (apple, orange, or strawberry slice) followed by three thick banana slices onto the skewer.

3 Slide three banana slices onto the skewer.

4 Use mini chocolate chips for buttons and eyes, add carrots for a nose, and press pretzel arms into each side of the center banana slice.

Sweet Notes

These Christmas cakes, cookies, candies, and other treats, all inspired by holiday songs and carols, may be the yummiest you've ever had.

Here Comes Santa Claus Cake

ACTIVE TIME 35 minutes, plus decorating
TOTAL TIME 1 hour, plus decorating
SERVES 20

FOR THE CAKE

- Butter, for pans
- 2 cups all-purpose flour
- ¼ cup unsweetened cocoa powder
- 1 teaspoon baking soda
- ½ teaspoon baking powder
- ½ teaspoon kosher salt
- 1½ cups granulated sugar
- 1 tablespoon red liquid food coloring
- 1 teaspoon pure vanilla extract
- 2 teaspoons white vinegar
- ¾ cup (1½ sticks) unsalted butter, at room temperature
- 2 large eggs
- 1 cup buttermilk

FOR THE FROSTING

- ¾ cup (1½ sticks) unsalted butter, at room temperature
- 8 ounces cream cheese, at room temperature
- 1 pound confectioners' sugar
- Red gel food coloring

FOR THE DECORATIONS

- Cornstarch, for work surface
- 4 ounces white fondant
- Gold food coloring spray
- 4 ounces black fondant
- 3 chocolate wafer cookies (such as Nabisco Famous Chocolate Wafers)

OTHER MATERIALS

- 13-by-9-inch cake pan
- Parchment paper
- Measuring cups and spoons
- 2 medium bowls
- Whisk
- Electric mixer
- Large bowl
- Oven mitts
- Wooden toothpick
- Wire rack
- Piping bag with large flat tip
- Offset spatula
- Knife
- Rolling pin
- 3-inch square cookie cutter (optional)
- 2-inch square cookie cutter (optional)

MAKE THE CAKE

1   Heat the oven to 350°F. Lightly butter a 13-by-9-inch cake pan, and line with parchment paper, leaving a 2-inch overhang on the two long sides; oil the parchment.

2   In a medium bowl, whisk together the flour, cocoa, baking soda, baking powder, and salt. Using an electric mixer, in a large bowl, beat the sugar, food coloring, vanilla, vinegar, and butter until light and fluffy, about 3 minutes. Beat in the eggs, one at a time. Reduce the mixer speed to low, and alternately add the flour mixture and buttermilk, mixing just until incorporated.

3   Spread the batter into the prepared pan, and bake until a toothpick inserted in the center comes out clean, 30 to 35 minutes. Let cool in pan for 15 minutes. Then use parchment overhangs to transfer to a wire rack, and let cool completely.

MAKE THE FROSTING

1   Using an electric mixer, beat the butter and cream cheese in a medium bowl on low speed until smooth. Beat in the confectioners' sugar on medium until fluffy, about 2 minutes.

2   Transfer 1 cup of frosting to a piping bag fitted with a large flat tip. Tint the remaining frosting red, and spread it evenly over the cake. Refrigerate until no longer tacky, 5 to 10 minutes.

TIME TO DECORATE!

1   Using the remaining frosting, pipe a 3-inch-wide strip down the center of the cake lengthwise. Smooth with an offset spatula.

2   Lightly dust a clean work surface with cornstarch. Roll out the white fondant, and use a 3-inch cookie cutter to cut out the belt buckle. Use the 2-inch square to cut out the center. Transfer to a sheet of parchment paper, coat with gold food coloring spray, and let dry, about 10 minutes.

3   Add more cornstarch to your work area if needed. Roll black fondant into a 9-by-3-inch rectangle, and place on the cake. Top with the belt buckle. Place two wafer cookies above the belt and one wafer below the belt for buttons.

Rockin' Around the Tree Cupcakes

ACTIVE TIME 15 minutes
TOTAL TIME 15 minutes, plus setting
MAKES 12

- 12 store-bought cupcakes with white frosting
- Finely shredded coconut (optional)
- Pretzel sticks
- 8 ounces dark-green candy melts
- Nonpareils, decorative sprinkles, and candies, including yellow stars

OTHER MATERIALS

- 2 large baking sheets
- Reusable silicone baking mats or parchment paper
- Medium microwave-safe bowl
- Oven mitts
- Mixing spoon
- Resealable plastic bag
- Scissors

1 For a snowy effect, sprinkle shredded coconut on top of each cupcake if desired.

2 Time to make your trees! Line two large baking sheets with silicone baking mats or parchment paper. Lay pretzel sticks (your tree trunks) on the sheets, allowing 2 inches of space between each one.

3 In a medium bowl, melt green chocolate melts in the microwave according to package instructions. Transfer the melted chocolate to a quart-size resealable plastic bag. Snip off one corner with scissors. Now you have a piping bag.

4 Squeeze the bag, and drizzle "greenery" onto the pretzel sticks. To make the Christmas tree shape, start with narrow back-and-forth drizzles as the top of the pretzel stick. Then make drizzles wider as you move down the stick. Leave a "trunk" at the end so the tree has room to stick into the cupcake.

5 While the chocolate is wet, trim the trees. Sprinkle with nonpareils and other decorative sprinkles and candies. Top with candy stars, and let set.

6 Once dry, carefully peel the mat or parchment paper from the back of the trees. Push a tree into each cupcake.

Hark! The Herald Angels Sing Cookie Garland

ACTIVE TIME 10 minutes, plus decorating

TOTAL TIME 55 minutes, plus decorating

MAKES 36 to 48 cookies (depending on shape and size)

- 1 batch Gingerbread Cookie Dough (page 115)
- All-purpose flour, for coating
- 7-ounce pouch white cookie icing
- Food coloring pens in various colors

OTHER MATERIALS

- Angel-shaped cookie cutter
- Reusable straw
- Oven mitts
- Wire rack
- Ribbon

1. Prepare cookie dough according to recipe instructions, using flour-coated angel-shaped cookie cutters to cut out cookies from the Gingerbread Cookie Dough. Use a reusable straw to punch a small hole into each angel's wing. Bake as directed, and let cool completely.

2. Time to decorate! Outline and fill in cookies with icing. Let set.

3. Once icing is set, use the food coloring pens to add details to the angels, like hair, faces, and dress details.

4. Finally, string together the angel cookies with ribbon for the perfect edible decoration.

Let It Snow Gingerbread Cookies

ACTIVE TIME 3 hours, plus decorating
TOTAL TIME 3 hours 30 minutes, plus decorating
MAKES 21 double snowflakes and 24 small snowflakes

- 1 batch Gingerbread Cookie Dough (page 115)
- All-purpose flour, for coating
- 32 blue hard candies (such as Jolly Ranchers)
- 7-ounce pouch white cookie icing
- Sanding sugar, for decorating

OTHER MATERIALS

- 2 large cookie sheets
- Parchment paper
- Large, medium, and small snowflake cookie cutters
- Oven mitts
- Wire rack

1   Line two large cookie sheets with parchment paper.

2   Prepare cookie dough according to recipe instructions, using flour-coated large snowflake cookie cutters to cut out cookies from Gingerbread Cookie Dough. Use a medium snowflake cookie cutter to cut the centers from the large snowflakes. Use a small snowflake cookie cutter to cut the centers from the medium snowflakes. Roll any excess dough, and cut more medium snowflakes.

3   Place all snowflake cutouts on a cookie sheet. Refrigerate until firm, at least 10 minutes.

4   Heat the oven to 350°F. Once the cookies are firm, crush the hard candies into fine pieces, and spoon them into the centers of the large and medium snowflakes (one candy per large snowflake and ½ candy per medium snowflake). Refrigerate for 10 minutes more.

5   Bake one sheet at a time, until the candies have melted and the cookies are just starting to brown, 7 to 9 minutes. Let cool on the tray for 5 minutes until the candies harden, then transfer to a wire rack.

6   Use small dabs of cookie icing to glue a medium cookie to the center of a large cookie. Decorate with additional cookie icing, and sprinkle with sanding sugar while wet. Let the cookies dry completely.

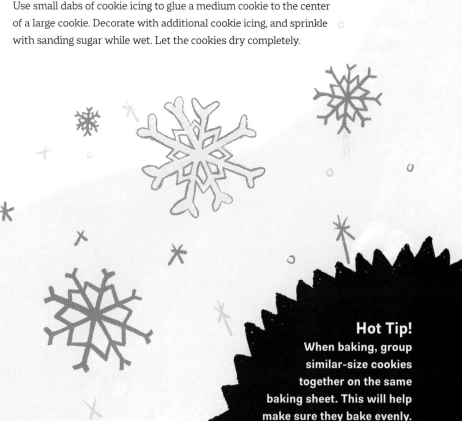

Hot Tip!
When baking, group similar-size cookies together on the same baking sheet. This will help make sure they bake evenly.

Jingle Bell Pops

ACTIVE TIME 50 minutes, plus decorating
TOTAL TIME 1 hour 35 minutes,
plus decorating
MAKES 12

- 8 ounces peanut butter or vanilla sandwich cookies
- 4 ounces cream cheese, at room temperature
- 2 cups white candy melts
- Silver and gold luster dust
- 1 teaspoon pure peppermint extract
- 7-ounce pouch black cookie icing

OTHER MATERIALS

- Food processor
- Parchment paper
- Baking sheet
- Measuring cups and spoons
- Glass measuring cup or bowl
- Oven mitts
- Lollipop sticks
- Floral foam
- Small bowl
- 2 paintbrushes
- Paper towel

1   In a food processor, pulse the cookies to form fine crumbs. Add small pieces of the cream cheese bit by bit to the processor, and pulse to combine. Roll the mixture into 1-inch balls, and place on a parchment-lined baking sheet. Refrigerate until firm, about 1 hour.

2   In a glass measuring cup or bowl, melt the white candy melts in the microwave according to package instructions. Dip lollipop sticks into the melts, then into each cookie ball; return the balls to the baking sheet, and refrigerate until set, about 5 minutes. (This holds the stick in place.)

3   Remelt the candy melts if necessary. Working with one cookie pop at a time (keep the rest in the fridge), dip the cookie balls into the candy melts, swirling to coat and tapping off any excess. Stick pops into the floral foam so they can set upright. Repeat with the remaining cookie balls, remelting the candy melts as necessary. Refrigerate until set, about 10 minutes.

4   In a small bowl, combine the silver luster dust and ½ teaspoon peppermint extract until it's the consistency of watercolor paint. Use a paintbrush to paint half the balls, letting them dry and repainting as necessary until they're fully covered. Let dry. With a dry paper towel, gently smooth the surface. Repeat with the gold luster dust and remaining balls.

5   Use the cookie icing to pipe an X onto the top of each cake pop.

Deck the Halls Holly Bark

ACTIVE TIME 15 minutes, plus decorating
TOTAL TIME 35 minutes, plus decorating
MAKES About 20 pieces of bark

- 28 chocolate sandwich cookies (such as Oreos)

- 2 pounds white chocolate candy melts

- 3 ounces dark-green candy melts

- Holly sprinkles or red nonpareils

OTHER MATERIALS

- 9-by-13-inch sheet pan or platter

- Nonstick foil

- 2 medium, microwave-safe bowls

- Oven mitts

- Offset spatula or butter knife

- Spoon

- Wooden skewer

- Cutting board

- Sharp knife

1   Line a rimmed 9-by-13-inch sheet pan with nonstick foil, leaving a 2-inch overhang on all four sides. Arrange the cookies in a single layer on the bottom of the pan.

2   In a medium bowl, melt the white candy melts in the microwave according to package instructions. Pour the melted chocolate over the cookies, filling the pan or platter and spreading with an offset spatula or a butter knife to smooth.

3   In another medium bowl, melt the green candy melts in the microwave according to package instructions. Before the white chocolate sets, spoon six green circles onto the white chocolate. Using a skewer, gently swirl the green into the white, so the circles look like wreaths.

4   While the chocolate is still warm, decorate with the sprinkles or nonpareils.

5   Refrigerate until set, about 20 minutes. Use the foil overhangs to transfer to a cutting board, and have an adult cut the bark pieces with a sharp knife.

Puppy Chow Mix

ACTIVE TIME 15 minutes
TOTAL TIME 15 minutes
MAKES 10 cups of puppy chow

- 8 cups square rice cereal (such as Chex)
- ½ cup creamy peanut butter
- 2 cups green candy melts
- 1 tablespoon vegetable oil
- 1½ cups confectioners' sugar
- 2 cups red and green candy-coated chocolates (such as Sixlets)
- 2 cups mini marshmallows

OTHER MATERIALS

- Measuring cups and spoons
- 2 large bowls
- Medium microwave-safe bowl
- Oven mitts
- Large resealable plastic bag
- Large bowl

1 Place cereal in a large bowl. In a medium bowl, microwave peanut butter, candy melts, and oil on high, stirring every 10 seconds, until melted. Carefully pour the mixture over the cereal, and toss gently to coat completely.

2 Transfer coated cereal to a large resealable plastic bag, and add confectioners' sugar. Shake the bag well to coat.

3 Pour the mixture into a large bowl, and let cool completely.

4 To serve, toss with red and green candies and mini marshmallows.

Peppermint Shakes

ACTIVE TIME 5 minutes
TOTAL TIME 5 minutes
MAKES 2

- 2½ cups vanilla bean ice cream, softened
- ¼ cup milk
- ¾ teaspoon pure peppermint extract
- Green gel food coloring
- Whipped cream, for serving (optional)
- Green and red sprinkles, for serving (optional)

OTHER MATERIALS

- Blender
- Measuring cups and spoons
- 2 glasses, for serving

1 In a blender, add ice cream, milk, peppermint extract, and three drops of green gel food coloring. Blend until combined.

2 Pour milkshakes into two glasses. Top shakes with whipped cream and sprinkles if desired.

Santa Claus Is Comin' to Town Candy Train

ACTIVE TIME 45 minutes
TOTAL TIME 45 minutes

Get on board and build this chocolate candy train, then load it up with more of your favorite candies. Look at the picture for inspiration to make tasty trees, presents, and passengers, or make your own candy creations. Use cookie icing to stick everything in place.

- 7-ounce pouch white cookie icing
- 12 snack-size white chocolate candy bars (such as Kit Kats)
- 16 starlight mints
- 20 chewy candies (such as Spree)
- 8 small mini-banana-shaped candies (such as Kooky Bananas)
- 1 white chocolate peanut butter cup (such as Reese's)
- 1 white chocolate mini peanut butter cup (such as Reese's)
- Your favorite candies as cargo or decoration (we used fruit slices, gumdrops, and spice drops)

OTHER MATERIALS

- Long, narrow serving platter
- Sharp paring knife

Sprinkles are easy stars!

This scrumptious Santa is made from **gumdrops**, **sprinkles**, and **icing**. Yum!

Try **spearmint leaf gummy candies** for trees. Trim their wider ends to make the bottoms flat.

TO MAKE THE CARS

1. Break white chocolate candy bars into two-piece bars. Stack them in threes, sticking them together with cookie icing, to form four stacks in a line on a serving platter.

2. Using cookie icing, attach two mints to both sides of each car for wheels. Attach one chewy candy to the center of each mint with a dab of icing, pressing to secure. Then use icing to stick a banana-shaped candy between each set of wheels.

FOR THE ENGINE

1. Trim ⅛ inch from one edge of a large peanut butter cup. Pipe icing on the bottom of the cup, and attach it, trimmed side down, to the front of the first car.

2. Attach a mini peanut butter cup on top of the car, near the front, with more icing.

Stack candies to make pipes and domes on your train.

Square fruit taffies like **Starburst** make colorful candy presents.

A **yellow gumdrop** could be a light.

The Little Drummer Boy Mini-Cakes

ACTIVE TIME 50 minutes, plus decorating
TOTAL TIME 1 hour, plus decorating
MAKES 12

- 1 box (16 ounces) store-bought pound cake mix
- Vegetable oil, for greasing
- 1 container (15 ounces) store-bought vanilla frosting
- Gold food coloring
- Red shoelace licorice
- Pretzel sticks

OTHER MATERIALS

- 12 mini cheesecake pans with removable bottom
- Oven mitts
- Small bowl
- Quart-size resealable plastic bag
- Scissors
- Offset spatula

1. Heat the oven to 350°F. Oil the cups of the cheesecake pans.

2. Prepare pound cake batter according to package directions. Divide the batter evenly among the cheesecake pans. Bake according to package directions. Let cool completely before frosting and decorating.

3. In a small bowl, tint ⅓ cup frosting with gold food coloring. Transfer the gold frosting to a quart-size resealable plastic bag. Snip off one corner with scissors, and set aside.

4. Using an offset spatula, frost the cakes with the remaining white frosting. Wrap the licorice around the top and bottom of each cake. Pipe on gold lines, and top with pretzel sticks.

A CUPFUL of FUN

Level up your hot cocoa game with these easy treats.

Simple Homemade Hot Cocoa

ACTIVE TIME 5 minutes
TOTAL TIME 20 minutes
MAKES 8 cups

- 2 cups unsweetened cocoa powder
- ¾ cup sugar
- 8 cups milk
- 8 ounces semisweet chocolate chips

OTHER MATERIALS

- Large saucepan
- Whisk

1 In a large saucepan, combine the cocoa powder and sugar on medium-low heat.

2 Whisk in 1½ cups milk until fully combined. The mixture will be a thick paste at this point.

3 Gradually whisk in the remaining 6½ cups milk. Add the chocolate chips, and whisk until melted. Serve immediately with marshmallows or whipped cream.

Snowman Marshmallows

ACTIVE TIME 10 minutes
TOTAL TIME 10 minutes
MAKES As many as you like!

- Dark chocolate candy melts
- Orange candy melts
- Standard-size marshmallows

OTHER MATERIALS

- Heatproof containers
- Toothpicks

1 Melt dark chocolate and orange candy melts in separate containers, according to package instructions.

2 Dip a toothpick into the dark chocolate melt and dab dots onto the flat surface of a marshmallow to create eyes and a mouth. Then dip a separate toothpick into the orange melt to swipe on a carrot nose.

3 Serve in your favorite hot chocolate, and drink quickly—before they disappear.

169

Hot Cocoa Mug Cake

ACTIVE TIME 5 minutes

TOTAL TIME 8 minutes

MAKES 1

- 1 tablespoon unsalted butter
- 2 ounces bittersweet chocolate, chopped
- 1 large egg
- 2 tablespoons light brown sugar
- 1½ teaspoons pure vanilla extract
- 2 tablespoons all-purpose flour
- 2 tablespoons cocoa powder
- ½ teaspoon baking powder
- Pinch kosher salt
- Whipped cream or whipped topping, for serving (optional)

OTHER MATERIALS

- 10- to 12-ounce microwave-safe mug
- Spoon

1 Place the butter and chocolate in a mug, and microwave in 20-second intervals until smooth; let cool for 5 minutes.

2 Add egg, sugar, and vanilla to the mug, and stir to combine. Then add flour, cocoa, baking powder, and salt to the mug, and stir to combine.

3 Microwave on high until still slightly underbaked in the middle, about 90 seconds. Serve with whipped cream or topping if desired.

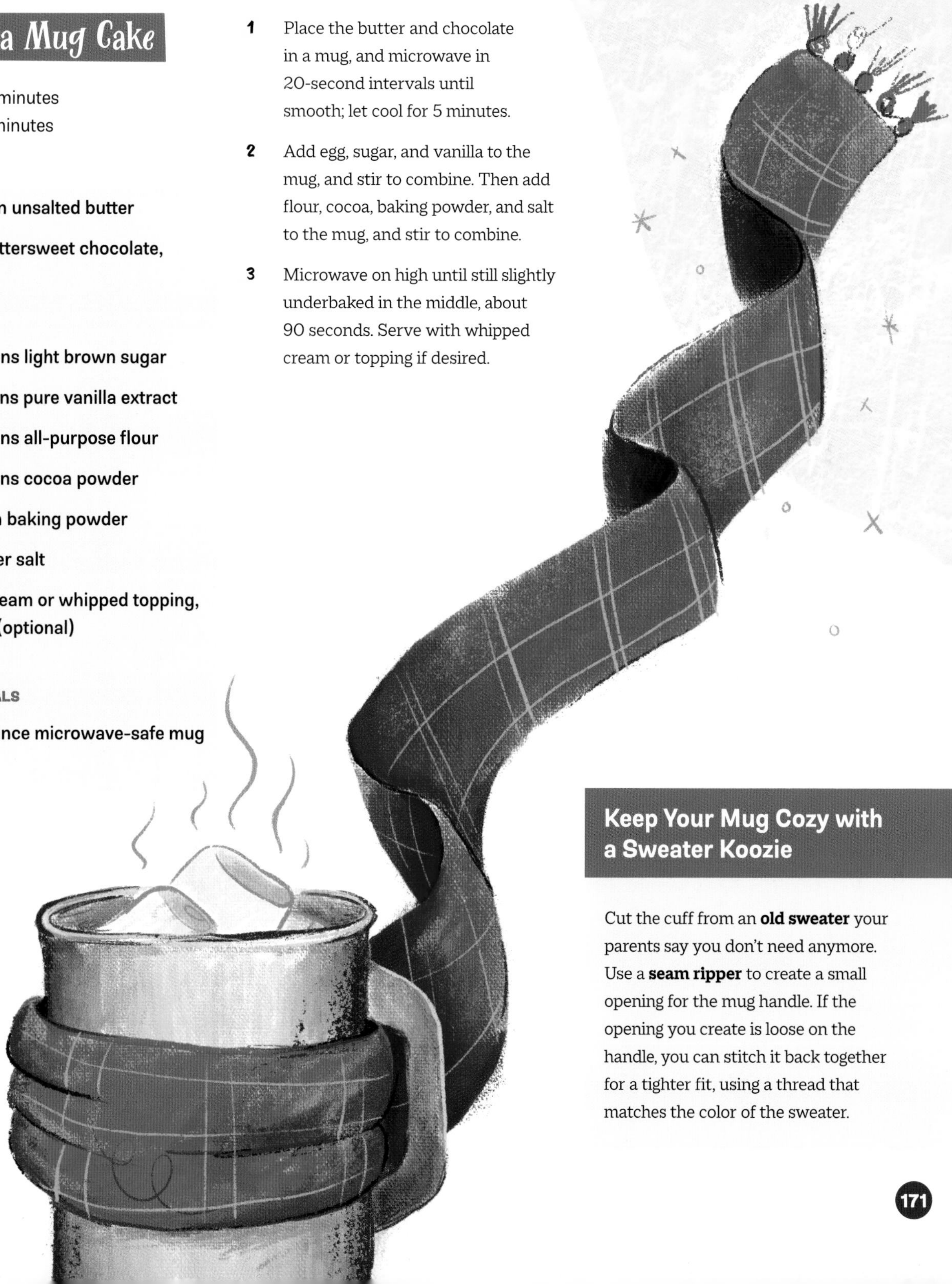

Keep Your Mug Cozy with a Sweater Koozie

Cut the cuff from an **old sweater** your parents say you don't need anymore. Use a **seam ripper** to create a small opening for the mug handle. If the opening you create is loose on the handle, you can stitch it back together for a tighter fit, using a thread that matches the color of the sweater.

Candy & Cocoa Kit

ACTIVE TIME 10 minutes

TOTAL TIME 10 minutes

MAKES 1

- **Green peppermint tree**
  (for a how-to on making these, see
  the Melted Ornaments on page 99;
  skip poking a hole in them with a
  wooden skewer since you won't be
  using them as an ornament)

- **¼ cup cocoa powder**

- **1½ tablespoons sugar**

- **1 marshmallow snowman
  (such as Peeps)**

- **1 cup very hot milk, for serving**

OTHER MATERIALS

- **Airtight glass jar**

1   Pour cocoa powder into the
    jar, then top with sugar.

2   Place the marshmallow and green
    peppermint tree in each jar.

3   When ready to enjoy, pour in
    hot milk. Stir to combine.

Gift It!
Tie a small ribbon around the lid.
Write the instructions from step 3 on
a gift tag so recipients can enjoy their
cup of cheer when they're ready.

Mix and Be Merry

Stir up some sweetness this season! Pour **melted white**, **milk**, or **dark chocolate** into spoons, then—before the chocolate melts—add **mini chocolate chips**, **toasted coconut flakes**, **crushed candy canes**, **sprinkles**, or **chopped mini marshmallows.** Let your decorated spoons sit for a few minutes until the chocolate has cooled and hardened. Wrap them in cellophane, and tie with twine or a ribbon for a fun gift for your friends and family. All they have to do is stir the spoons into warm milk for a delicious treat.

Love at First Sip

Hot cocoa has been stirring up fans for quite a long time—more than 2,500 years, as a matter of fact! The Mayans, who lived in present-day Mexico and Guatemala, as well as parts of Belize and Honduras, are believed to have created the first chocolate drink around 500 BCE. It was made from ground-up cocoa seeds mixed with water, cornmeal, and chile peppers. Eventually, the drink was introduced in Europe, where the spice was swapped for sugar.

Fun & Festive Faces

From charming elves to happy penguins, these cheery treats are sure to put a smile on your face as well.

Santa & Elf Cookies

ACTIVE TIME 30 minutes, plus decorating
TOTAL TIME 1 hour, plus decorating
MAKES 36 to 48

FOR THE COOKIES

- 1 batch Classic Sugar Cookie Dough (page 113)
- 1 batch Black Cocoa Cookie Dough (page 114)

FOR THE FROSTING AND DECORATIONS

- 7-ounce pouch white cookie icing
- 7-ounce pouch red cookie icing
- 7-ounce pouch gold cookie icing
- Additional bags of cookie icing for extra details (optional)
- Sanding sugars and other sprinkles, for decorating

OTHER MATERIALS

- Triangle cookie cutter
- Mustache and beard cookie cutters (optional)

1   Prepare cookies according to recipe instructions, using a flour-coated triangle cookie cutter to cut out cookies from the Classic Sugar Cookie Dough and a cocoa-coated triangle cookie cutter to cut out cookies from Black Cocoa Cookie Dough. Cut out beards and mustaches with flour- or cocoa-coated mustache and beard cookie cutters if using.

2   Use the icing pouches to transform cookies into elves and St. Nicks. To make hats and coats, outline and fill in cookies with icing. Let sit for 3 minutes, then sprinkle with sanding sugar for a little sparkle. Apply the same technique to the mustaches and beards. Let set, and add swirls if desired. Use the cookie icing and sprinkles to add faces.

3   Attach the mustaches and beards with a dab of cookie icing.

A PERFECT
TREAT FOR
YOUR
DEEREST
FRIENDS!

Reindeer Cream Puffs

ACTIVE TIME 30 minutes
TOTAL TIME 1 hour
MAKES 12

- 12 store-bought cream puffs, thawed
- Dark chocolate melts
- Milk chocolate melts
- White sprinkles
- Red or brown candy-coated chocolates (such as M&M's)
- 16-ounce container store-bought buttercream-style vanilla frosting

OTHER MATERIALS

- Parchment paper
- Pencil
- Baking sheet
- 2 small microwave-safe bowls
- Oven mitts
- 3 piping bags
- 2 medium round piping tips
- Small star piping tip

1. On a piece of parchment paper, sketch antler shapes. Place on a baking sheet, writing side down.

2. In a small bowl, melt dark chocolate melts according to package instructions. Carefully transfer melted chocolate to a piping bag with a medium round tip. Trace the antlers with piped chocolate directly on the parchment paper. Let set.

3. In another small bowl, melt milk chocolate melts according to package instructions. Carefully transfer melted chocolate into another piping bag with a medium round tip. Pipe the milk chocolate directly onto the cream puffs to create reindeer heads and eyes. Immediately add white sprinkles to the heads for spots and press candy-coated chocolates on for noses. Gently push the set antlers into the tops of the cream puffs. (Check out the picture for reference.)

4. Place buttercream in a piping bag fitted with the small star tip. Pipe your reindeers' ears right in front of the antlers.

Ice Bear Cupcakes

ACTIVE TIME 1 hour
TOTAL TIME 1 hour 30 minutes
MAKES 12

- 12 store-bought cupcakes with white frosting
- 12 mini chocolate-covered donuts (such as Entenmann's Mini Rich Frosted Donuts)
- 12 donut holes
- 32 marshmallows
- 24 gumdrops
- 16-ounce container store-bought buttercream-style vanilla frosting
- Finely shredded coconut, for coating
- 7-ounce pouch black cookie icing
- Cornstarch, for work surface
- 4.4-ounce package red fondant
- Brown candy-coated chocolates (such as M&M's)

OTHER MATERIALS

- Butter knife
- Toothpicks
- Paring knife
- Kitchen scissors
- Frosting spatula
- Rolling pin
- Ruler

1   Using a butter knife, scrape most of the frosting off the store-bought cupcakes so only a thin layer remains.

2   Top each cupcake with an upside-down donut. Stick one end of a toothpick into each donut hole, and attach it to the cupcake by sticking the other end through the center of the donut resting on the cupcake.

3   Make the noses: Using the paring knife, carefully slice off and discard the top third of 12 of the marshmallows. Insert a toothpick into the cut side of each marshmallow, and attach them to the donut holes.

4   Make the ears: Cut 12 toothpicks in half with kitchen scissors. Attach each to a gumdrop, and insert the other end into the donut holes. (Place them above the marshmallows so they're where the bears' ears should be.)

5   Use an offset spatula to cover the cupcake and attachments (marshmallow, gumdrops, and all) in vanilla frosting, then coat the frosting in coconut to give your bear its furry texture.

6   For the paws, use the paring knife to cut slices off the outsides of the remaining marshmallows. Use black cookie icing to pipe on paw pads and claws. Let set, then attach to bears using additional vanilla frosting.

7   Lightly dust a work surface with cornstarch, and use the rolling pin to roll out the red fondant. Use the ruler and paring knife to measure and cut 6-by-¼-inch strips of fondant for scarves, and snip the ends with kitchen scissors to create fringe. Wrap the scarves around the bears' necks.

8   Use vanilla icing to attach a brown candy to the front of the face for the nose, then pipe a mouth, eyes, and eyebrows with the black cookie icing.

Before eating a cupcake, carefully disassemble and remove any toothpicks before taking that first bite.

Nutcracker Mouse King Pie

ACTIVE TIME 15 minutes, plus decorating
TOTAL TIME 15 minutes, plus decorating and chilling
MAKES 6 slices

- 9-inch store-bought pie, such as cheesecake or fudge
- Chocolate candy wafers (such as Necco Chocolate Wafers)
- Mini brown candy-coated chocolates (such as M&M's)
- Mini dark chocolate nonpareils (such as Sno-Caps)
- Crown-shaped gold sprinkle

OTHER MATERIALS

- Sharp knife
- Serving platter

1   Have an adult cut the pie into six slices with a sharp knife. Place pieces on a serving platter, leaving yourself plenty of room to decorate each piece.

2   Make each Mouse King by gently pushing a wafer into the wide corners of each slice. Then press on candy-coated chocolates for eyes, nonpareils for noses, and sprinkles for crowns.

Sandwich Cookie Penguins

ACTIVE TIME 1 hour

TOTAL TIME 1 hour

MAKES 12

- 12 chocolate sandwich cookies (such as Oreos)
- 3 tablespoons shredded coconut
- 12 mini chocolate sandwich cookies (such as Oreo Minis)
- 7-ounce pouch white cookie icing
- Candy eyes
- Yellow candies (such as Banana Runts), halved

OTHER MATERIALS

- Butter knife
- Measuring spoon

1   Carefully separate the standard sandwich cookies, keeping the cream filling intact.

2   To make each penguin body, use your fingers to gently press ½ teaspoon of shredded coconut onto the cream filling. Discard the halves that don't have cream on them.

3   Carefully separate the mini sandwich cookies. Using a butter knife, scrape off and discard the cream filling. Set aside 12 whole pieces for the penguin heads, then cut the remaining 12 pieces in half for the wings.

4   Using cookie icing, stick two candy eyes and one halved yellow candy on one whole mini piece to create a face. Repeat for the rest of the whole mini cookie pieces. Attach the faces to the cookie bodies with a dab of cookie icing.

5   Complete each body by using the cookie icing to attach two half mini cookie pieces for the wings and two halved yellow candies to the coconut-covered cream for the feet.

Nutty North Pole Cookies

ACTIVE TIME 20 minutes
TOTAL TIME 2 hours, or until icing sets
MAKES 24

- 7-ounce pouch red cookie icing
- 7-ounce pouch white cookie icing
- 7-ounce pouch green cookie icing
- 24 peanut butter sandwich cookies (such as Nutter Butter)
- Finely shredded coconut
- Sliced almonds
- Candy eyes

OTHER MATERIALS

- Toothpick

1   Using cookie icing, outline the hats, clothes, beards, and faces of your North Pole characters on the peanut butter sandwich cookies. Fill in the hats and clothing, using a toothpick to drag icing to the edges. Let the icing dry between colors.

2   For a fluffy beard, sprinkle finely shredded coconut onto white icing while it's still wet.

3   Use the icing to attach sliced almonds for the elves' ears.

4   Finish your holiday helpers by sticking candy eyes to the elves with small dabs of icing.

Need to Avoid Peanuts?
These goofy faces will work on other sandwich cookies and sugar cookies too!

Polar Bear & Fa-La-La-La-Llama Cookies

ACTIVE TIME 30 minutes, plus decorating
TOTAL TIME 1 hour, plus decorating
MAKES 36 to 48 (depending on shape and size)

To make these trees, wrap sour strap candy around foam cylinders, attaching with a toothpick in the back.

- 1 batch Classic Sugar Cookie Dough (page 113)
- 7-ounce pouch white cookie icing
- Mini brown candy-coated chocolates (such as M&M's)
- 7-ounce pouch black cookie icing
- Additional pouches of colored cookie icing, for decorating

OTHER MATERIALS

- Bear-shaped cookie cutter
- Llama-shaped cookie cutter

1   Prepare cookie dough according to recipe instructions, using flour-coated cookie cutters to cut out bears and llamas. Bake as directed, and let cool completely.

2   Time to decorate! Outline and fill in cookies with white icing. Let dry.

3   To make polar bear muzzles and llama faces, pipe a mound of white cookie icing in one spot. Let sit until almost dry, then press on mini candies for the polar bears' noses. Pipe on eyes, noses, mouths, and eyebrows with black cookie icing.

4   Finish these sweet friends by piping on sweaters, scarves, and hats using the additional colors of cookie icing.

SCAN HERE!

Snow Angels

ACTIVE TIME 2 hours 40 minutes
TOTAL TIME 3 hours 50 minutes
MAKES 36 to 48

- 1 batch Black Cocoa Cookie Dough (page 114)
- 7-ounce pouch white cookie icing
- Additional bags of colored cookie icing, for decorating
- White sanding sugar
- Confectioners' sugar, for serving

OTHER MATERIALS

- Printed snow angel–shaped cookie templates (scan the smart code)
- Scissors
- Paring knife
- Serving platter

1. Use scissors to cut out the printed snow angel-shaped cookie templates.

2. Prepare cookie dough according to recipe instructions. Using the paring knife, carefully trace around the templates to cut out snow angel-shaped cookies. Bake as directed, and let cool completely.

3. Use the white icing to pipe faces onto the angels. Let the icing dry completely before switching colors. Then, working one color at a time, use the bags of cookie icing to pipe hair and clothing onto the angels. For a sparkly finish, sprinkle your decorations with sanding sugar while the icing is wet.

4. Up the fun by dusting a serving platter with a thick layer of confectioners' sugar. Place the decorated cookies on the sugar, pressing down and twisting slightly to make angel shapes in the "snow."

SO VERY THANKFUL

Words of thanks to those who were kind enough to give you presents or spend time with you during the holidays will be the best gift they receive. Follow this example for the best-ever thank-you card.

1 Including the date you wrote the letter gives the note a time stamp—a nice little touch in case someone saves it to look back on it years from now.

2 Keep it casual! Open your note using the name you call the person day-to-day.

3 Cut to the chase. A simple "Thank you" is the perfect opener.

4 Mention the gift or act of kindness specifically.*

If you received money or a gift card, you do not have to include the amount but might say "generous" or "thoughtful" check or gift card.

5 Describe how you'll use the gift! If you're thanking the person for an experience, tell them about your favorite part of the time you spent together.

6 A simple summary line is a good way to wrap things up.

7 Hey, everyone loves to receive a little compliment!

8 Close in a way that reflects your relationship: "Love" for family or good friends.

9 A handwritten note is always a nice gesture. But if you type it out, sign your name.

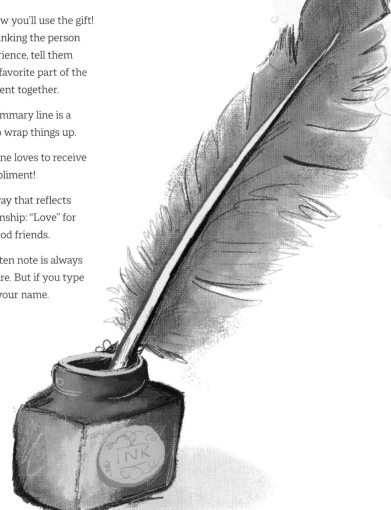

JANUARY 6

DEAR GRANDMA,

THANK YOU FOR MY WONDERFUL
CHRISTMAS GIFT. I LOVE THE NEW
ART SET, AND AM LOOKING
FORWARD TO PAINTING A
PICTURE OF OUR CAT, JINGLES,
TO HANG IN MY ROOM.
I APPRECIATE YOUR THOUGHTFUL
PRESENT. YOU'RE THE BEST!

LOVE,

JACK

Recipe Index

Index

Credits

Illustrations: Russell Shaw

Cover: Russell Shaw

Alex Potemkin/Alamy: 141;
Alison Gootee: 63; **David Tsay:** 42;
Emily Kate Roemer: 68;
James Schaedig/Alamy: 45;
Joni Hanebutt/Alamy: 141;
Jonny Valiant: 166; **Marcus Nilsson:** 138;
Paul Whicheloe: 107;
The Omni Grove Park Inn: 141;
WeLoveWreaths.com: 75

Adobe Stock: 22, 27, 29, 32, 33, 34, 36, 38,
46, 48, 53, 84, 112, 114, 142, 187

Alexandra Rowley: 119, 129, 149, 182, 183

Antonis Achilleos: 69, 108, 170

Becky Stayner: 54, 118, 130, 168

Brian Woodcock: 41, 80, 92, 95, 96, 98,
101, 102

Con Poulos: 146, 148, 150, 180, 185

**Courtesy of Heidi Tyline King /
www.heiditking.com:** 91, 106

Danielle Daly: 62, 70, 71, 72, 74, 86

David Hillegas: 64, 67, 76, 79, 88, 90, 105

Erika Lapresto: 71, 73, 78

Getty Images: 45, 141

Kate Sears: 107, 116, 128

Mike Garten: 70, 83, 89, 120, 122, 126, 132, 134,
136, 143, 144, 149, 162, 164, 165, 172, 176

Steve Giralt: 124, 152, 154, 156, 158, 160, 169,
174, 178, 184

Written by Caroline McKenzie

Book design by Russell Shaw

Library of Congress Cataloging-in-Publication Data Available on request

10 9 8 7 6 5 4 3 2 1

Published by Hearst Home, an imprint of Hearst Books/Hearst Communications, Inc.
300 W 57th Street
New York, NY 10019

For information about custom editions, special sales, premium and
corporate purchases: hearst.com/magazines/hearst-books

Printed in China
ISBN 978-1-958395-99-8

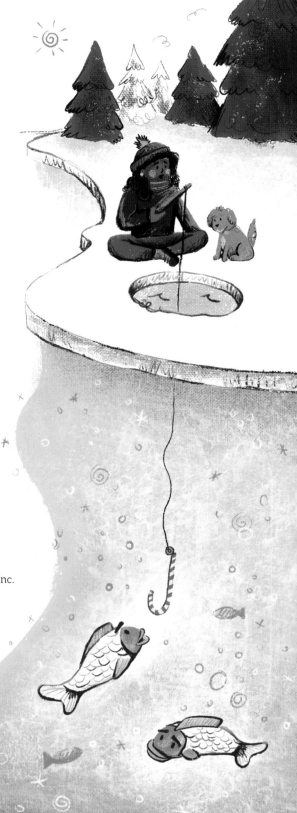